$2
Lumor
0810

D1381037

A
Diabolical
Dictionary
of
Education

Books by Richard Armour include:

Prose

American Lit Relit
Armour's Almanac
The Classics Reclassified
A Diabolical Dictionary of Education
Drug Store Days
English Lit Relit
Going Around in Academic Circles
Golf Is a Four-Letter Word
It All Started with Columbus
It All Started with Europa
It All Started with Eve
It All Started with Hippocrates
It All Started with Marx
It All Started with Stones and Clubs
My Life with Women
A Safari into Satire
Through Darkest Adolescence
Twisted Tales from Shakespeare
Writing Light Verse

Verse

An Armoury of Light Verse
For Partly Proud Parents
Light Armour
Nights with Armour
The Medical Muse
Punctured Poems

For Young People

The Adventures of Egbert the Easter Egg
Animals on the Ceiling
A Dozen Dinosaurs
Odd Old Mammals
On Your Marks: A Package of Punctuation
Our Presidents
The Year Santa Went Modern

Educationally illustrated by

Henry Syverson

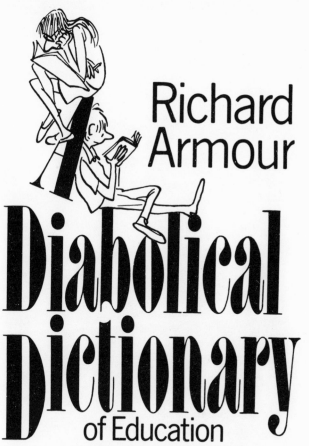

Richard Armour

Diabolical Dictionary

of Education

An absolutely dispensable guide
through the muddle and maze of the
American school system for students,
teachers, parents, and others who seek a
better understanding of educational terms
than they will get here

The World Publishing Company
New York and Cleveland

Published by The World Publishing Company
2231 West 110th Street, Cleveland, Ohio 44102

Published simultaneously in Canada by
Nelson, Foster & Scott, Ltd.

First Printing—1969

Copyright © 1969 by Richard Armour

Illustrations copyright © 1969 by Henry Syverson

All rights reserved. No part of this book may be
reproduced in any form without written permission
from the publisher, except for brief passages included
in a review appearing in a newspaper or magazine.

Manufactured at World Publishing Press, a division
of The World Publishing Company, Cleveland, Ohio

Library of Congress Catalog Card Number: 70–92533
Printed in the United States of America

WORLD PUBLISHING
  TIMES MIRROR

Dedicated to teaching,
the second-oldest profession

Preface

Writing a dictionary such as this is risky business. Ambrose Bierce, the author of *The Devil's Dictionary*, went to Mexico in 1914 and has not been heard of since. He may have been shot by Pancho Villa. He may, foolishly, have drunk the water. He may still be alive, at the age of 127, hiding out to avoid a libel suit.

Despite the hazards of legal action, exile, and murder, I have felt it necessary to write this book. After thirty-eight years of teaching without a teacher's credential or, indeed, without having taken a single course in Education, I consider myself eminently qualified. I am absolutely without prejudice. Some of my best friends are educators.

An educator and a teacher, I should point out, are not necessarily the same. As "educator" is defined by an educator, "it implies a quality of achievement or performance higher than usual." How high usual is, the educator, who may have been a little high himself when he wrote this, does not say. But an educator is apparently, in educational terminology, an overachiever as compared with a mere teacher. He falls only a little short of an educationist, a specialist in educational theory, an educator of educators.

As can be seen already, you cannot understand education today unless you have at least an elementary knowledge of Educationese, the language spoken in educational circles. This language, created largely by educational psychologists, is rich in compounds such as "pluralsignificant" and "homoscedasticity," the latter being lucidly defined as "the property of a double-entry table composed of arrays all of which have equal variability." The language of educators may also be recognized by such sonorous phrases as "humanized guidance instruction," "transfer of abstract relationships," and "intergroup education in cooperating schools."

There are certain basic principles in Educationese. ("Basic," of course, is never "basic" but always "basal.") One is that a short word is never used if a long word is available. Another is that if a long word is not available one can be invented. Still another is that anything that is understandable at first reading needs to be revised. If there are no four-letter words in Educationese, this is not because of moral scruples but because four-letter words usually come from Anglo-Saxon, while the words used in Education are derived from Latin and Greek. Did you ever hear anyone say, "It's all Anglo-Saxon to me"?

Unlike most dictionaries, this one is small and selective. It may not be the kind of book you cannot put down, but it is the kind of book you *can* pick up. If a few important words are omitted, it is because some, like "modal divergence," the author was unable to understand and therefore somewhat hesitant to explain, while others, like "dysdiadochokinesia," he was afraid he might be asked to pronounce.

On the other hand, at the risk of being charged with incompleteness and superficiality, the author did not include, as did the compiler of one dictionary of education (a Professor of Education and onetime high school principal), such a word as "building." In this rival dictionary, "building" is defined as "an edifice or structure having outside walls and a roof, enclosing space for use, but not a structure on wheels or one designed to float on water; presumed to be permanently attached to the ground and considered as belonging to the real estate."*

* This is the truth. The reader will find no untruths or half-truths in this book, but occasionally a truth and a half.

It is hoped that the present dictionary will provide not only a definition of words used, misused, and overused in the field of education but also some insight into what is going on in our schools and colleges. The informed reader will not demand that a principal be dismissed and run out of town because he called an attractive young teacher into his office and forced her to show him her credentials. Nor will the reader who has kept this dictionary for ready reference make the embarrassing mistake of asking, "Where is the department head?" when he is looking for the men's room.

Education has come a long way since James A. Garfield, ten years before he became President of the United States, declared: "Give me a log hut, with only a simple bench, Mark Hopkins on one end and I on the other, and you may have all the buildings, apparatus, and libraries without him." The one-to-one teacher-student ratio is no longer possible, science teachers need more than a simple bench to perform laboratory experiments, and librarians like to be able to bring books in out of the rain. Garfield, listing the educational paraphernalia he could get along without, failed to mention trustees, presidents, deans, superintendents, principals, school boards, etc., all of which are in this book and can be skipped by any taxpayer who shares Garfield's love of simplicity.

As education has developed, so has the language of those in the profession: people do not speak but communicate and they use "id" more than "it." Some, though they have not dropped out, have dropped behind. It is for them that this dictionary was written. Once they have perused such entries as "clay behavior," "interpersonal relations," and "dynamic substrata-factor theory of reading," they will have a new confidence, a new sense of belonging, and be able to throw their weight around at the next meeting of the AAUP or PTA.

Remember that great American, Millard Fillmore. A poor

lad who could only infrequently be spared from his father's farm, he had little schooling. But he brilliantly made up for this lack: he married his teacher. A fine example of Instant Education. For students who are too young to marry their teacher and for teachers who are too old to marry their students, this dictionary will prove a reliable substitute.

R.A.

A
Diabolical
Dictionary
of
Education

A. The highest grade. A grade given by some teachers to every student in the class, especially teachers of art and those about to retire who should have retired years ago. Also a grade never given by certain teachers, known by students as "hard," "sadistic," and "inhuman." A+ is slightly better than perfect and is indicative of emotionalism on the part of the teacher. A— is a grade given to show (a) a small amount of dissatisfaction or (b) skepticism about there being any such thing as perfection.

AAUP. American Association of University Professors. An organization of professors that blacklists a college when it dismisses a professor for some such reason as poor teaching, alcoholism, or being involved with a student in a paternity suit. A college or university on the AAUP blacklist may be forced to recruit its faculty from ex-convicts, mental patients, or, as a last resort, persons without a Ph.D.[1]

[1] The AAUP itself says it "censures" rather than "blacklists," perhaps fearful of being charged with racism.

ABD. All but dissertation. This describes the status of those who have completed course work, qualifying examinations, and residence requirements and would have their doctorate if they could just finish their dissertation, which they have not yet started. To be so close to their degree (within eight or ten years) is frustrating. If they just could work full-time. . . . If they just had a subject. . . . If they just could write. . . . If they just had gone into business. . . .

Aberration. In education, any deviation from the norm, the norm being established by someone who is considered (by himself) to be normal. This may be why so many superintendents and principals are named Norman and called Norm by their friends.

Ability expectancy. The highest level of development a student may be expected to reach, considering his intelligence and industry, if nothing unusual happens, such as having a good teacher who takes an interest in him.

Academic. Theoretical, not expected to produce any practical result, as in "strictly academic," "academic question," and "academic freedom."[1] From the Greek *akademeia*, a garden or grove near Athens where Plato and his followers walked around and around, never getting anywhere.

Acceleration. Placing certain students in more advanced classes. This enables them to go from work that is too easy to work that is too difficult. Students who keep up with the acceleration are through school and out

[1] For impracticality, at least for everyday use, consider academic regalia. Try keeping on a mortarboard in a high wind.

in the world before they understand what they have learned. In this connection, see "to accelerate," to step on the gas, which also can be educational.

Achievement-oriented. The main purpose of this type of teaching is to help the student achieve his goal, which is usually to get through school and start doing something useful, such as earning money. Parents understand and applaud this kind of education.

Achievement test. A test of (1) what the student has achieved, (2) what the student may be expected to achieve, (3) the ingenuity of the educational experts who contrived the test. There is always the possibility that at the time of taking the test the student was ill or under the influence of drugs. The same may have been true of the educational experts who prepared the test, especially when they came up with a question like "If you have twelve apples and sell three for ten cents each, how long would it take to eat those that remain?" There are two types of achievement test: (1) objective and (2) objectionable.

Achiever. *Obs.* See "overachiever" and "underachiever."[1]

ADA. (1) Americans for Democratic Action. (2) American Dental Association. (3) Average Daily Attendance. This is what determines tax apportionment and therefore is of life-and-death importance. A student who is absent for some reason other than illness is not

[1] In some other dictionary.

counted, brings in no tax money, and might as well be dead.

Administrator. A person who once taught but now is paid more for doing less.[1] In colleges and universities an administrator, unlike a professor, has no tenure, which means that he could be dismissed at the end of the academic year if it were not for his friends on the Board of Trustees.

Admission. (1) Getting in. (2) Acknowledgment of an error or acceptance of a previously unaccepted fact. *Rare.*

Adult education. (1) Education of adults. (2) Education that is not childish.

Advanced placement. A form of acceleration, so flattering that it compensates for any feeling of inferiority occasioned by being forced to drop out after a few weeks and return to the regular class, which by this time is itself too far advanced to catch up with.

Advanced standing. Much like "advanced placement" except that the student does more standing, especially when there is a shortage of classroom space or the chairs were borrowed for a football rally.

Application. (1) Filling out forms that were prepared by the same educational experts who prepared the achievement test, the only clear instruction being "Sign here."[2] The applicant lists as references the

[1] Or, as the years go by, less and less.
[2] The applicant can get back at them by signing his name illegibly.

17

names of persons thought to be favorably disposed or under some obligation to Dad. (2) The act of fixing the mind closely, attentively. *Rare*, at least in the classroom.

Aptitude test. A test intended to reveal a student's ability for performance of a certain type of activity. A student who scores low in mathematics may score high in English, and then again he may not. One way to test aptitude for music is to seat a child at a piano and leave him there for several days. If, at the end of that period, he is found picking out a simple tune, such as a Chopin sonata, he would appear to have a certain aptitude for music. If, on the other hand, he has climbed into the piano and detached the wires and got them into an impossible tangle, he probably has the mechanical aptitude to become an automobile repairman.

Arts and crafts. An area of activity in which the principles of art[1] are applied to such worthwhile fields as metalwork, leatherwork, ceramics, and woodcarving. Instead of being merely ornamental, art becomes useful, and a home can be full of creatively designed coat hangers, doorstops, and paper-clip containers. Ashtrays can become so beautiful that guests will drop ashes into their pockets rather than defile them, thus making it easier for the housewife.

Athlete's foot. An infection of the feet caused by a ringworm fungus that the school physician (trying to frighten his patients) calls *Tinea trichophyton.* Fear of getting athlete's foot is one reason why a cer-

[1] To be distinguished from the art (or craft) of principals.

18

tain high-school student refused to go out for football. Another reason was that he weighed only 120 pounds.[1]

Attention span. Length of time a student can concentrate on something. The attention span will be found to vary greatly, depending on what the student is concentrating on. A high-school student who can concentrate on a textbook only for seconds can concentrate for hours on his image in a mirror or the centerfold photo in *Playboy*. One of the most wistful and forlorn statements of a teacher is "Let me have your attention, *please!*"

Audiobus. A teaching aid on wheels; a bus fitted with tape-recorded lectures and with a headset for each student. Students are thus able to learn while riding to and from school and on field trips, though they lose much of the old fun of throwing books out of the window and playing tricks on the driver, such as smearing peanut butter on his back. It is also hard to run up and down the aisle with a headset attached. When the audio-videobus comes into use, students

[1] He also bruised easily.

will no longer go to school. They will simply go to and from school. The only people at school will be teachers, busy putting on makeup, turning their good profile to the camera, and answering fan mail.

B. To an optimist, a grade just below A; to a pessimist, a grade just above C. Considered by the registrar the equivalent of Good, though instructors who give nothing higher consider it Excellent and those who give nothing lower consider it a Bare Pass. Professors who give all B's are invulnerable. Unlike those who give all A's, they are not criticized for being too easy and letting down standards. Yet they never have to justify a C, D, or F to a complaining student or parent.

Baccalaureate. The bachelor's degree, conferred also on married men. Women, too, receive the bachelor's degree, though for some a spinster's degree would seem more appropriate. The abbreviation of bachelor of arts is B.A., which, as few of those on whom it is conferred know, stands for *Baccalaureus Artium. Baccalaureus* itself comes from *baccalaris*, a tenant farmer or shepherd, and this in turn is derived from *baculum*, a staff. Some etymologists think it is also related to *bacterium*, and in view of the pale, sickly look of some graduates they may be right.[1]

Baccalaureate sermon. A feature of the commencement exercises in which graduates (see the reference to *bacterium*, above) are given last rites and extreme unction, usually by an extremely unctuous preacher.

Basal reader. Not to be confused with basal metabolism. A basal (basic, to those not in education) reader is a textbook used for instruction in reading. Anything learned from it in addition to how to read is highly unlikely.[2]

Behavioral sciences. Though not accepted as sciences by scientists (e.g., organic, inorganic, and outorganic chemists), the behavioral sciences include such fields as sociology and anthropology. When sociology became known as a behavioral science, the sociologists moved into a new building, leaving English and philosophy behind. Behavioral scientists are concerned with the behavior of man, and well they might be.

Bibliography. A list of books placed at the end of a term paper to impress the teacher. Not included is the one book the student actually used, probably the *Encyclopaedia Britannica*.

[1] Wild though some baccalaureate exercises may be (see "Baccalaureate sermon," below), there seems to be no justification for relating the word to "Bacchus" and "bacchanalian."

[2] Students may also learn how to care for a book even though, when asked how they liked the book, they may say, "I didn't care for it."

Board. (1) A school board. (2) A blackboard. A white blackboard is rare, but not so rare as a black school board, especially in Mississippi.

Browsing room. A room with armchairs, footstools, good lighting, and books that can be read without having to be remembered. Students in the browsing room are either so bright that they have finished their work, so dumb that they are flunking out anyhow, or in need of sleep. A few students may just like to read good books.

Buddy system. Pairing of two children in hazardous activities such as swimming or nature-study hikes, each child being supposed to look after the other. The buddy system has proved conclusively that two can drown or get lost as easily as one.

Budget estimate. Estimate of funds needed for the next school year and having little or no relationship to funds actually forthcoming. Typical items in a school budget estimate are these:

Water coolers	$9,200
Aluminum athletic supporters[1]	$22,875
Social studies teacher	$6,600

Bulletin board. A board to which are fastened announcements, menus, offers to swap (books, cars, roommates, etc.), lost articles, job opportunities, and photographs of wanted persons. A typical opening with possibilities for rapid advancement is that of a

[1] An athletic supporter can, of course, be an old grad who turns up at all the games, cheering wildly.

dishwasher in the school cafeteria, who may expect to move up within a year from pots and pans to cups and saucers. The bulletin board is also known as a tackboard, since there are more people who put things up than take them down, and it usually looks tacky. The word "bulletin," by the way, comes from the Italian *bulletino* and is the diminutive of *bulla*, an edict of the Pope or a Papal bull. A bulletin, then, is a little bull, as anyone knows who has read the notices on a school bulletin board.

Bus capacity. The maximum number of students that a school bus can carry safely and comfortably, or at least safely. The capacity of a school bus is determined by measuring the seating space and allowing 13 inches per student. Since students are usually standing or jumping up and down, the measurement should perhaps be of their feet, not their seat. The only person who remains seated at all times is the driver, and he is ready to jump off at any moment. Instead of keeping his eye on the road, he keeps his eye on the mirror. If you heard those strange noises and felt the bus swaying, wouldn't you want to know what was going on behind your back?

Business English. An area of study involving English used in business. Students learn such colorful expressions as "Yrs of the 15th inst. rec'd and contents noted."[1]

[1] The efforts of Chinese merchants to pronounce "business" gave rise to the word "pidgin." Business English is therefore, in a way, pidgin English, which will come as no surprise to anyone who has ever studied or taught it.

Bussing. (1) Transporting black children to white neighborhoods and white children to black neighborhoods. If all the black children were bussed to a school in a white neighborhood and all the white children to a school in a black neighborhood, segregation could be maintained and black children and white children could wave at each other as they passed, thus creating good feeling without fear of intermarriage. (2) Kissing. *Obs.* That is, the term "bussing" for kissing is obsolete, but not kissing.

C. Referred to as a gentleman's grade, especially by young men who say they could make a higher grade if they worked harder. Persons who question this are not being very gentlemanly.

Cafeteria. A place where students eat lunch. The food, prepared by a dietitian, all has the same taste, but one dish can be distinguished from another by the color and shape. A balanced meal is one that is placed on a tray and carried to a table without spillage.

Calendar. Unlike the ordinary calendar, the academic calendar has only nine months and begins in September instead of January. Important days on the academic calendar are not Christmas, Easter, and

24

Washington's Birthday but Classes Begin, Low Grade Reports, and Final Examinations. There is competition among groups to get an event on the calendar. For instance, the Dance Society and the German Club may both want March 12th, and the secretary in the President's Office who is in charge of the calendar must be impervious to flattery, bribes, and threatening phone calls.

Campus. As it was originally used by the Romans, the word *campus* meant an open space or field employed for martial exercises, public shows, etc. Except for such martial exercises as ROTC drills and the even more martial demonstrations against them, a campus is now merely the grounds between college or school buildings, with KEEP OFF THE GRASS signs which form back-rests for students lying on the grass.[1]

Career day. A day when representatives of various businesses and professions come to the school to discuss career opportunities with students. If they represent a company that makes a war-related product, such as helmet liners or powdered milk, they may find themselves locked in a closet for three days without food or water, or chased onto the roof, where they have a choice of staying or jumping. They will be lucky if they are burned in effigy and not in person. The representative of a conglomerate, owning so many and such diverse companies that the moral issue is blurred, may be so fortunate as to get an uninter-

[1] See Gertrude Stein's "Students on the grass, alas." The "alas" may be a typographical error, and she may have meant "a lad and a lass."

rupted interview with a student. If so, the student may momentarily put aside his picketing sign, DOWN WITH THE MILITARY-INDUSTRIAL COMPLEX, and ask such discerning questions as "What's the starting salary?" and "How about fringe benefits?"

Carrell. A cubicle (not to be confused with a cuticle, which is only slightly smaller) in the library. The carrell is something like a phone booth without a phone. It has no door, but is wide open at one side, thus improving ventilation and making it possible for anyone passing by to see who is in there and what he is doing. By their senior year students learn to sleep with their eyes open. The library carrell is year around, unlike the Christmas carrell.

Chair. (1) A seat for one person that usually has four legs and a back and may have arms. (2) An endowed professorship, occupied by a professor who has two legs, a back, and arms. A professor who has his own chair has more prestige and gets a higher salary than his colleagues. This helps create the typical atmosphere of a community of scholars: one filled with jealousy, distrust, and hatred. A chair usually bears the name of the donor, someone who might have had his name on a building had he been willing to dig a little deeper.[1]

Chalk. A soft limestone of earthy texture, white, gray, or buff in color, chiefly composed of the minute shells of *Foraminifera*. Few teachers, unless their subject is Geology, realize that they are scratching on the board

[1] A rocking chair would be appropriate for a professor emeritus.

with the remains of a Cretaceous rhizopod. Teachers who do much writing on the board are well advised not to wear navy blue suits or dresses. Writing with chalk on the board was probably the first visual aid, and is gradually being replaced by overhead projectors and other more expensive devices. When a piece of chalk breaks in two, it is still usable, and there is no need to call for a chalk repairman and wait around several hours for his arrival.

Chalkboard. A term increasingly used instead of "blackboard," especially in schools where *Little Black Sambo* has been removed from reading lists by groups otherwise vigorously opposed to censorship.[1]

Classroom control. Keeping an iron hand over students, and occasionally letting it drop on someone's head. Actually control must be achieved by other than physical means, such as psychological ploys, sex appeal (especially in young female teachers), hypnotism, bribery, and blackmail. More difficult than, and related to, classroom control is self-control, pretending to be relaxed and unconcerned while seething within. After all, students cannot be removed without trouble with parents, but ulcers can, and there is nothing like the blissful quiet of a hospital room.

Clay behavior. A technique whereby a child is given clay to play with, and what he does with it is observed in studying aesthetic creativity. He may, for instance, throw it at the wall, thus indicating a feeling for nonrepresentational modern art. Similar techniques are cup-and-cube behavior, cup-and-spoon behavior,

[1] Chalk is often green or yellow, but chalk talks are never blue.

draw-a-man behavior, paper-folding behavior, etc. One of the most interesting is negative behavior, when the child's activity takes the form of inactivity. There is also good behavior. *Rare.*

Coach. A former athlete, now reduced (though twenty pounds overweight) to teaching boys football or, if he teaches in a private school, football, baseball, basketball, soccer, swimming, tennis, golf, track, squash, and lacrosse. If the coach gets more excited than anyone else at a game, it is because one more loss means his job.

Coathletics. Athletic activities in which students of both sexes participate together. Because of censorship laws in some states, this will not be discussed here.[1]

Coeducation. Men and women attending the same institution. Since women students are called coeds, men

[1] There was some thought of a mention in the appendix, but the appendix was removed.

should be called eds, but they are not, unless they are named Ed. In some institutions men and women live in the same dormitory, in different wings or on different floors. (Not many actually live *on* the floor, except in Japan.) If what is called permissiveness continues, and men and women live in the same rooms, coeducation will become cohabitation, and women will be known as cohabs.

Cognitive response. A term preferred by those in the field of Education to knowing, understanding, catching on. It may come unexpectedly from a student who has given no indication of possessing intelligence, or even a brain, when a casual reference is made to the student's area of interest, such as the major-league batting averages.

Collateral reading. Reading done on the side, though it may also be done on the back or stomach. Collateral reading is usually suggested rather than assigned, and by doing such reading a student indicates either (1) enthusiasm for the subject, or (2) hope of making a favorable impression on the teacher.[1]

Commencement. A ceremony marking the end of such hardships as physical education, institutional food, and a roommate of the same sex. It also marks the beginning of a new life of freedom to support oneself. The high point of the ceremony is when the commencement speaker, all too long after commencing, concludes.

[1] By not doing such reading, a student shows himself to be normal.

Most Athletic

Most Popular

Class Clown

Most Likely to Succeed

Communication gap. (1) Failure of a teacher to understand the incoherent mumbling of a student and failure of a student to listen to what the teacher is saying. (2) Gap between the front teeth of a child, making all letters sibilants, especially aggravated when the teacher's name is Miss Sybil Sorenson. (3) Gap between knee and skirt that leaves even professors of Speech speechless. (4) Gap about which everyone communicates endlessly, saying things like "What we have is a communication gap," "But for the communication gap," and, in really rough company, "It's the d-mned communication gap." This might be the time to mention, if ever, that one definition of "communication" is "intercourse by words, letters, or messages." No wonder so many find it unsatisfactory.

Continuing education. Education for older women who dropped out of college because they were pregnant or graduated from college but are unable to understand their children's fourth-grade homework. Such persons find the return to study difficult at first, but think this is only because they are rusty. Gradually they discover that they have lost the ability to concentrate and remember.[1] Though they do not continue their continuing education, they continue to plan to do so some day.

Corporal punishment. (1) Punishment of a noncommissioned officer. (2) Punishing a student by slapping, beating, whipping, mauling, tearing limb from limb, or doing any of the other things that fill a

[1] Or realize they never had it.

teacher's daydreams. Unfortunately corporal punishment is frowned upon, and in some districts scowled upon, by the School Board and by parents who are saving this sort of thing for recreation at home. In some rural school districts, the student is so much taller and heavier than the teacher that though this type of punishment is not discouraged, the teacher is.

Counselor. A giver of advice that is taken only when it is what the student intended to do anyhow.[1]

Counseling center. A place where counselors, psychiatrists, ministers, and other specialists meet disturbed students. The sign on the door saying DO NOT DISTURB has special significance. At the end of a normal day of abnormality the custodian sweeps up bitten-off fingernails, torn-out hair, and discarded egos and ids. Now and then he takes home a superego to show his wife. "This is the biggest one I've seen yet," he says.

Cram. To cram is to study intensively, cramming facts into the brain, during the last hours before an examination. Cramming too soon is a waste, since by the time of the examination everything learned will have been forgotten. Cramming just before the examination ensures that important facts will be remembered until just after the examination. Aids to cramming are a fellow crammer, hot coffee, cold showers, pep pills, and fear.[2]

[1] What we have always wondered is who counsels counselors.
[2] Interestingly, "cram" spelled backward is "marc," which indicates its relationship to getting a good marc or grade.

Curriculum. From the Latin *curriculum*, a racecourse or a chariot, which in turn comes from *currere*, to run. From this we also have the curricle, a two-wheeled chaise drawn by two horses abreast. As it is used today, curriculum refers to the body of courses offered by an educational institution, but the original meaning has not been entirely lost. Teachers involved in a curriculum have the feeling of running around and around a race track but never getting anywhere. Some, after a hard day, feel as if they have been pulling a curricle, with the superintendent, principal, and two members of the School Board inside, urging them on.

Curve. Grading on the curve means (1) giving a certain number of A's, B's, C's, D's, and F's, regardless of how smart or dumb the class is, thus permitting a teacher to establish the mean grade and the students to refer to the teacher as a mean grader; (2) a teacher, behind with paperwork, grading while driving, perhaps on a mountain road.[1]

Custodian. Formerly known as Janitor. May in time be called Vice-President in Charge of Buildings. Custodian is from the Latin *custodia*, which in turn is from *custos*, guard, and is akin to the Greek *keuthein*,

[1] Of him it may be said, "He never made the grade."

33

to hide. A custodian may hide, all right, especially when he is urgently needed to unlock a door or bring in some extra chairs. Mostly, though, he sweeps the floors, cleans the blackboards, and empties the wastebaskets. Lost articles are kept in his office, which also serves as a broom closet. A school could get along without the principal and any five teachers more easily than without the custodian. He knows more about the students than anyone else, partly from notes he has run across when emptying wastebaskets. From the same source he has enough on teachers to augment his retired pay with blackmail if he chooses to do so. If he sifts through the contents of wastebaskets rather thoroughly, before consigning papers to the furnace, it is because of his hope of running across the sketches of a future Leonardo or the theorems of another Einstein, partly obscured by a wad of gum.

D. Lowest passing grade. While some students are unhappy at getting a D, others breathe a sigh of relief and say, "Well, I squeaked through." Everyone agrees, however, that a D is not a very good grade. Of course subjective factors sometimes play a part— such as a teacher's having taken a dislike to a student because he comes to class late, cracks his knuckles, and once worked in the personnel office and checked the records and discovered the teacher's true age. Then again, a soft-hearted teacher may give a student a D— instead of an F, especially when the student's father is a member of the Board of Trustees.

Dawning-realism developmental stage. In art education this is when a child becomes aware of physical differences between boys and girls and begins to make those differences apparent in his drawings. A boy may not understand why a teacher confiscates the drawing of a girl that he was showing everybody, the one he copied from a magazine his father left in the bathroom. He may not know art, but he is beginning to know what he likes.

Dean. From the Latin *decem*, ten, because a dean, or *decanus*, was originally the head over ten monks in a monastery. Today there are many deans: Dean of the Faculty, Dean of Men, Dean of Women (Dean of

Boys, Dean of Girls), and Dean of Admissions, who spends his time admitting the school's errors.[1]

Dean's list. (1) A list of students making a certain grade average. (2) A list of groceries the dean's wife gave him that he tucked away in his pocket and forgot.

Demonstration. (1) Showing students how to do something. Thus a teacher might demonstrate the law of gravity by jumping out of a third-story window. (2) Picketing, boycotting classes, and shouting slogans such as "No more tests!" "A's for everybody!" and "Teachers are pigs!" In this type of demonstration it is the student who demonstrates to the teacher how it is done, and soon the teacher is out marching with a sign reading "More pay, less work," "Shorter hours, better students," or "Better hours, shorter students."

[1] Our sympathy goes out to deans whose first name is Dean, as well as to deans whose last name is Dean and persons in academic life whose first name is Dean but are not deans.

A demonstration is said to get "slightly out of hand" when someone sets fire to a building or occupies the president's (or principal's) office, holding the poor fellow hostage and not even letting him call his wife, who is upset because dinner is on the table and getting cold.

Department. Actually a compartment, within which is confined all the teaching of a subject as well as all the learning of it, if any. A department may have a rotating chairman (spinning dizzily) or a head. A department head is not to be confused with the lavatory restricted to members of the department, each of whom has a key which he wears on a chain instead of a Phi Beta Kappa key.[1] The main purpose of a department is to have more majors and a larger book budget than any other department and to keep the knowledge of one field from seeping into another, thus creating a situation that would be dangerously interdepartmental. It might be interesting to imagine Socrates, Erasmus, or Leonardo da Vinci in a department, perhaps in the same department, arguing about credits, prerequisites, and secretarial assistance.

Depersonalization. The teacher deals with a student without thinking of him as an individual, or even as a human being, which in some instances may be easy. Complete depersonalization may be achieved with the issuance of a hood to each student, a start having been made in psychology classes where one student

[1] With a little filing down and touching up, a key to the faculty washroom can be made to look like a Phi Beta Kappa key and a Phi Beta Kappa key, useful at last, can be made to open the washroom door.

preserves his anonymity by attending class in a sack. Some think depersonalization began when a teacher made a sarcastic remark and a student snarled back, "Don't get personal."

Depth learning. A learning process that enables students to get in deeper and deeper, until finally what they are studying is over their heads.[1]

Dewey decimal system. A secret code that permits librarians but no one else to find a book, thus making it necessary to hire trained librarians and insuring the continued existence of library schools. A struggle has developed between librarians using old-fashioned cataloguing methods and the proponents of computerized information retrieval systems. Fighting with their backs to the wall (or to the card catalogue), librarians, mindful of Dewey, cry, "Remember the Main!" Main Library, that is.

Dialogue. Formerly discussion, conversation, colloquy, or just plain talking together. In colleges and universities, students are especially eager for a dialogue with the administration, the dialogue usually taking the form of ultimatums from the students and evasive answers from the administration. Dialogues are supposed to open minds and close communication gaps. Sometimes, however, when they end in fisticuffs, they open cuts and close eyes.

Dingdong theory. The theory that language originated with reflex expressions caused by sensory impressions.

[1] This may have serious consequences in Introductory Swimming.

A good example of this is the word "ouch" or, after a distasteful sensory impression, the word "ugh," accompanied by a shudder. However, it is a little difficult to see how this theory accounts for a word like heteroscedasticity. The dingdong theory, by the way, gets its name from the analogy with the sound of a bell induced by the stroke of the clapper. There is also the bowwow theory, which maintains that language began with the imitation of natural sounds, such as the barking of dogs and the chirping of birds. Nor should we overlook the pooh-pooh theory, which holds that language originated with interjections that gradually acquired meaning.[1] By going into this sort of thing, a teacher can stall his way through a class period when he has not read the assignment he gave the students. Otherwise he may have to fall back on a snap quiz, which is more obvious.

Directed reading. Reading along suggested lines. If the lines, say in a poem by Allen Ginsberg, are not only suggested but suggestive, little direction may be necessary.

[1] Some skeptics pooh-pooh the pooh-pooh theory.

Discipline. *Obs.* See "Classroom control."

Dismissal. The same as discharge, but without a firearm. A teacher who is dismissed is usually asked to submit his resignation, which he has every reason to believe will be accepted. In fact he is probably resigned to the situation, though he may say, threateningly, "I'll hire a lawyer" or "I'll expose those sex deviates on the School Board," just before he suddenly leaves town.

Dissertation. An extended thesis, long enough to discourage anyone from reading it, which is one of the requirements for a Ph.D.[1] The purpose of the dissertation is to prove not only the student's stamina but his ability to find a subject in which no one has the slightest interest. He must then write about it in the distinctive prose style that is the hallmark of the scholar, i.e., wordy, wooden, and ungrammatical. If, in addition, each page is divided about equally between text and footnotes, and the bibliography includes works in French, German, and Urdu, the dissertation will be hailed as "a contribution to knowledge." The graduate student who can type, or who has a wife who can, even if she can't cook, is the envy of those who must pay by the page, with extra for carbons.

Dress code. Regulations concerning clothing worn to school. Most of the attention, especially on the part of male principals, is directed to the length of girls' skirts, though extremely low-cut blouses are not beneath, or above, notice. In the early days, a ruler was

[1] Members of the student's committee are forced to read the dissertation, or a few passages they can haggle over.

used by teachers to rap unruly students over the knuckles. Now, however, it is used to measure exposed flesh, starting at the knee, and is not broken as often as formerly. The right of students to wear whatever they wish is defended by many parents and by the ACLU, which cites the Second Amendment and the right to bare arms and no telling what else.

Driver education. Instruction in how to drive a car, resulting ultimately in the parents having to walk. A Ph.D. in Driver Education has not as yet been awarded, but the day is not far off.

Due process. Touching all the bases. Any administrator who fails to touch all the bases in firing a professor or expelling a student is out.[1]

Dynamic substrata-factor theory of reading. As explained simply and lucidly by an authority on the subject, it is: "A theory proposing that reading is a dynamic and complex act compounding and recompounding for each new and/or different reading task an appropriate integration of a multiplicity of related and underlying subabilities; some key concepts postulated are an integrating principle, a functional equipotentiality, cognitive working systems of subabilities, predominant use of preferred modes (tac-

[1] He is out of his mind if he thinks he can get away with it, what with the AAUP, ACLU, AFT, and NEA. There is no such organization as the SPCA (Society for the Prevention of Cruelty to Administrators).

tile-kinesthetic, motor, auditory, and visual) of functioning in different learning situations, maturational gradient-shifts, and the constant interaction of the whole and its parts." (Carter V. Good, ed., *Dictionary of Education*, p. 443.)

Dyslexia. Reading difficulty caused by visual aphasia or, indeed, any reading difficulty, since the word "dyslexia" mystifies parents and gives teachers a feeling of professionalism and intellectual superiority. Good use can also be made of dyslalia, dyslogia, dysphasia, dysphemia, dysphonia, dysplasia (as in "I hope this won't dysplasia"), dyspraxia, and dysrhythmia.[1]

Early room. A room provided for children who arrive before school starts. Such children are either eager to get going or are dropped off by their mother as she goes to work on the early shift at the local steel mill. Teachers who have trouble getting up should not be assigned to supervise activities in the early room.

Ed.D. Doctor of Education, a degree that permits the holder to be called "Doctor" but to operate only in the field of Education.

Educand. A person being educated. Also known, by persons not in the field of Education, as a pupil or

[1] And, of course, dyspepsia.

student. "Educand" deserves to be placed in the new category of *Abs.* (*Absurd*), along with "educational mortality" (dropping out) and "psychological life space" (environment).

Education. From the Latin *educatio*, originally the process of nourishing or physically rearing a child or young animal.[1] Today, however, the main distinction is between "education" and "Education," the latter being concerned with methodology but not necessarily with students. Graduate schools of Education teach teachers to teach and sometimes teach teachers to teach teachers to teach. Courses for those who would teach include "The Assessment of Deviate Characteristics of Children," with an M.D. and a policeman as guest lecturers, and "Research in Identity Formation in Adolescents," which includes field trips from which a would-be teacher sometimes fails to return.[2] Graduate students working for their P.P.S.C. (Pupil Personnel Services Credential) must undergo at least one supervised experience in a secondary school counseling center, in which they counsel a student while being watched by a senior professor known unpopularly as Big Brother. They are permitted a towel to use for mopping the perspiration from their brow and to throw on the floor if they are unable to take it any longer.

Educational psychology. Application of the methods and principles of psychology to educational problems.

[1] There at one time being a distinction between a child and a young animal.
[2] He may never be found, or he may be discovered in a bar, mumbling incoherently.

There is a world of difference between an educational psychologist and an educated psychologist, as one can tell by reading a few sentences in a journal of educational psychology.

Elementary. (1) Simple, easy, as in "Elementary, Dr. Watson." (2) Complicated, difficult, as in the teaching of the lower (elementary) grades.[1] In order to be qualified, a teacher must obtain an elementary teaching credential. This is obtained by taking at least thirty hours (and they seem like years) of work in such fields as the History of Education, School Law, judo, and karate. Since requirements differ in the various states, a Professor of Political Science at Harvard would not be permitted to teach fifth-grade Civics in Smiths Ferry, Idaho, without taking special courses. He might, of course, be granted the Temporary Certificate that enables bored housewives and high-school dropouts to take a crack at it.

Emerging self. Growth of the self through experience. Even bad experiences are good, because you learn from them and the self grows. As the self gets bigger and bigger, it eventually has to emerge from its cramped quarters. If you have pains, it may be the self trying to get out. Once the self is fully grown, it starts affecting other selves (i.e., society). Napoleon and Hitler are two examples of overgrown selves that affected millions of others. Students should be told such things, perhaps with some such admonition as "Watch your self!"

[1] Children in the lower grades are not (necessarily) low-grade children.

Emeritus. A title given to a retiring professor, along with a gold watch,[1] a scroll, a gift certificate at a hearing-aid store, and an endless dinner at which all the older emeriti fall asleep. "Emeritus" comes from the Latin *e + meritum*, meaning "out of merit," which is what the retired professor now is. An emeritus professor is not allowed to teach, but he is permitted to putter about in the library, where he can pretend to be writing the book that he was always going to write when he got the time.[2]

Endogenous feeble-mindedness. Inherited feeble-mindedness, as distinguished from exogenous feeble-mindedness, which includes all the other kinds. Despite irresponsible statements by enraged parents, both types are rare among teachers, except during an acute teacher shortage.

Endowment. The accumulation of money given to a private college by donors. Donors are to a private institution what taxpayers are to the government, except that they cannot be fined or jailed for failing to give. A college's endowment is invested to produce income. Income may be defined as what is never quite enough to pay current expenses. What is called "making up the difference" is something done each year by the trustees, who are encouraged to bring their checkbooks to the June meeting. A woman who is well endowed is different from a college that is well endowed. She is—well, endowed.

[1] A curious gift in that he no longer has any need to be on time anywhere.

[2] The watch, mentioned above, may be a subtle reminder that he now has the time.

Environmental factors. These include blackboard, desk, window, door, floor, ceiling, and anything else that may affect the student favorably or unfavorably, even a tic in the teacher's left eyelid. Psychologists have recently discovered that an important part of the word "environmental" is "mental." Nutritionists point out that it contains "iron," which is good for young, growing bodies. Experiments such as writing with black chalk on white blackboards and hiring prettier teachers may improve the learning environment. Incense and background music are also being considered.

Exchange professor. A professor who is exchanged for another professor, each professor thinking he is getting the better of it, or at least getting a change of scene. In exchanging professors, the rate of exchange is two associates or three assistants for one full. An exchange professor has no committee work, no dues for the local chapter of AAUP, and sometimes, if he is really lucky, no students.

Excuse slip. A slip containing a statement written by the student or his parents[1] to explain his absence or tardiness. Some excuses are rather lame, which is why the student is well advised to come to school on crutches.

Extended day. By holding classes also at night it is possible to extend the day for several hours, thus proving the superiority of state laws over natural laws. The extended day program gives students the opportunity to work full-time and yet go to school, provided they cut down on such nonessentials as

[1] Or by the student *for* his parents.

eating and sleeping. To most teachers, the old-fashioned unextended day seems long enough.

Extracurricular. Usually found in the expression "extracurricular activities." Such activities, being outside the curriculum, receive no academic credit, but who cares? They include wrestling (either in the gymnasium or in a parked car), drinking, picketing, heckling speakers, and designing and hanging effigies. One advantage of extracurricular over curricular activities is that they are not required and it is not possible to get an F. The failing student suffers only momentary embarrassment when cut from the baton-twirling squad.

Eye-rest period. A period devoted to activities other than those involving close eye use, to avoid eyestrain. Students may be told to look out of the window, even though that is what they have been doing all day, or they may be encouraged to roll their eyes, but not on the floor. After the eye-rest period students usually see better, especially if they put on their glasses.[1]

F. Grade signifying failure, often causing a drastic change in the student's educational plans. It would be even harder to bear if the student knew that F is also a voiceless labiodental fricative. An F can some-

[1] A bone-weary teacher may wish she could say, along about two-thirty of a Friday afternoon, "I rest. Period," and lay her head on her opened classbook and drop off to sleep.

times be made up to a D through hard work, bribery, or blackmail.

FF. A failure that cannot be made up. As low as you can go, there being no such thing as an FFF. A double F is the academic equivalent of death.

Felt needs. (1) Need for felt. (2) Belief of progressive education people that the curriculum should be determined by self-selection, in other words according to what the child thinks he needs. "Now what shall we study?" a teacher asks her third-grade class, and hopes no budding philosopher or voyeur answers, "Our navels."

Field trip. (1) Stumbling over something in a field. (2) Visit of a class to look at flowers (botany), rocks (geology), nudes (art), people (sociology). Specimens are more likely to be brought back in geology than in sociology. Field trips in English and philosophy are rare.

Film strip. (1) Film used as a visual aid in teaching. (2) Educational film, used in sex education, when actors and actresses remove their clothing a little at a time in order to explain things to slow learners.

Financial aid. Money given to students who, in the old days, would have waited tables or mowed lawns. If it is a loan, it is at a low interest, and the student also has a low interest in ever paying it back. The amount of financial aid is determined by a formula applied to the parents' assets and earnings, and if wealthy parents try to get the maximum aid, this only shows the kind of drive and determination that made them wealthy.[1]

Fine. (1) Excellent. (2) Charge made at library for books kept more than two weeks even though unopened. Also payment required by campus police when a student parks his car in a space clearly marked "Faculty" or a member of the faculty parks his car in a space clearly marked "Administration." A fine may be paid in cash or worked off by raking leaves. Faculty members usually prefer to pay cash or charge it to their department budget under "Miscellaneous."

Fire drill. Practice of orderly evacuation of the school building in case of fire. It is highly unlikely that there will be a fire, unless the fire insurance has lapsed, and even more unlikely that the evacuation would be orderly. Fire drill in many schools has been replaced

by disaster drill, which prepares everyone for action in the event of a disaster, such as a visit by the superintendent. Instead of trying to get out of the building, everyone tries to get into the basement, under

[1] If an interview is required, such parents park their Lincoln Continental a couple of blocks away and walk to the appointment, perhaps carrying a sack lunch in a polka-dotted bandanna at the end of a stick.

a desk, or behind a curtain. Teachers, having longer legs and stronger motivation, usually get there first.

Flow chart. Chart showing the flow of administrative responsibility or the sequence of steps in performing a task. In education, as in any field, a flow chart does not have to be followed, but it gives an office a look of purposefulness if hung on the wall alongside humorous, original signs such as THE BUCK STOPS HERE and THIMK. One other thing about flow charts: when whatever is flowing starts flowing backward, there is likely to be trouble, and it is a good idea to call a specialist, perhaps a plumber.

Formal education. Systematic education in a school. There is really nothing so formal about it, and teachers who turn up in dinner jackets and evening gowns will feel a trifle conspicuous. Oddly, education outside the classroom is not called informal education but learning-by-doing, learning the hard way, and attending the School of Hard Knocks. (Not to be confused with Knox College, in Galesburg, Illinois.) Experience, we are told, is the best teacher, perhaps because Experience never stays home with a cold or strikes for higher wages. Wordsworth had still another idea. "Let Nature be your teacher," he said, having in mind what you learn when you sit on a cactus plant or fall off a cliff.

Foundation. (1) A lady's undergarment.[1] (2) A tax-free corporation set up to do good, the founder having done well and feeling a little guilty about the

[1] At one time, but no longer, unmentionable, even in the classroom.

way he tricked his competitors and exploited his employees. Young men who enjoy giving more than receiving, especially giving money earned by others, should consider becoming foundation executives.

Frame of reference. An arbitrary set of axes, usually orthogonal, with reference to which the position or motion of a point, body, or group of bodies is described, or with reference to which physical laws are formulated. Teachers who use this expression several times an hour are probably thinking of something else, if at all.

Friday. The day before Saturday and Sunday. A book has been written entitled *Friday, Thank God!* It was written by a teacher, of course. A teacher is also said to have written a book about Monday, but no publisher would touch it.

Gang shower. Many misinterpret this, thinking it means that a number of students take a shower together in order to save water. Actually a gang shower is one for which the temperature of the water in all showers is set by a central valve. The water in each shower is therefore the same temperature, in other words a little too cold or a little too hot for the individual user. Some think the gang shower is Communist-inspired.[1]

Graduate record examination. An examination to determine whether a student has the knowledge and ability to go on to graduate school. The most important consideration, whether he also has the money, is not included among the questions. If he is intelligent enough to go to graduate school, he will have married someone who will take a job and support him while he studies.

Grant. (1) Civil War general, later President. (2) Sum of money given by the government or a foundation to make it possible for a popular, effective professor to stop teaching and do research. If the professor's research leads to publication, the result of the grant may be that the professor will gain an administrative ·position and thus never need to return to teaching. Part of the research, of course, will be an exhaustive study to attempt to discover whether the grant is tax deductible.

Gross teacher turnover. (1) Total turnover of teaching personnel in a certain period. This means all teachers, not simply the gross ones. Turning over a teacher is a delicate business, the more so if the teacher is uncooperative. (2) In some parts of the world, where cannibalism is practiced, such a turnover is a kind of semicircular pie or tart made by turning one half of

[1] It does not, however, reflect the Marxian idea of "to each according to his need."

a circular crust over the other, enclosing the fat teacher or the more edible parts thereof.[1]

Group dynamics. Shared feelings and interstimulative relationships of individuals in a group. By meeting

together in such a relationship, students may collectively develop a concept, such as that of setting fire to the Administration Building, that they would not have thought of by themselves. Another advantage of these meetings is that they prepare for sharing emotions later in such adult groups as Alcoholics Anonymous and the PTA.

"Guess who" technique. Students are shown photographs or descriptive sketches or listen to recordings of voices and are asked to identify the subject. "Guess who," the teacher says merrily, making a game of it. This is one time it is fun to be a teacher, knowing the answers and feeling very wise and superior. Once, though, when a teacher said, "Guess who," one of the boys came back with "Guess what. I don't want to play."

Guidance. Directing a student toward a goal. Not quite the same as telling a student (or a principal) where he can go.

[1] As a cannibal friend of mine says, "Don't knock it if you haven't tried it."

53

Guidance outcome. Result of guidance. "Guidance income," on the other hand, is the salary received by a teacher or counselor for giving guidance.

Hall pass. Authorization for a student to be in the hall instead of in class. Something like being out on parole. The money value of a hall pass, even a rather crude forgery, has increased astronomically in recent years.

Head start. Selected children from underprivileged or disadvantaged environments are given preparation before they enter the first grade. In education, giving someone a head start is considered perfectly all right, but in a track meet or a horse race this sort of thing would lead to disqualification. Anyhow, the head start idea in education is not to win but to tie.

High school. (1) School on top of a hill or in a tall building. (2) Expensive school, probably private. (3) School where students are on marijuana or pep pills.[1] (4) Exclamation, usually written "Hi, school!"

Home pickup. Transportation that picks up each child on the public highway in front of his home. The child is not actually picked up, but is expected to be stand-

[1] Or on glue, which is almost as bad as being in it. In either case, students find it hard to get loose.

ing there and to get into the school bus on his own, however reluctantly. It tugs at the heartstrings, watching children out in front of their homes waiting for the big yellow school bus. One minute they are there, set out on the curbstone like so many trash cans; the next they are gone, carried off to the dump (school). Unlike trash cans, however, they are not emptied but filled, though this is hard to tell just by looking at them.[1]

Home room. A room in which students start the day and to which they return from time to time to recuperate from the rigors of classes. The home-room teacher tries to make the students feel at home by calling the roll and seeing to it that everyone goes to the bathroom (but not at the same time). The home-room teacher is a sort of substitute mother and in some instances both mother and father, a role played especially well by a woman teacher with a low voice and hair on her upper lip. Students who act just as they would if they were at home are the home-room teacher's greatest problem.

[1] The difference between the school bus and the school bully is that the school bus picks *up* a small child, while the school bully picks *on* a small child, the smaller the better.

Homework. Work assigned by teachers (1) to keep the kids off the street in the afternoon and (2) to test the problem-solving ability of parents. (See "Continuing education.")

Honorary degree. A degree awarded for some exceptional achievement, such as giving the money for a new building. Take the case of Phystostomos Asafoetidon, LL.D., the shipping magnate who made possible the new Behavioral Sciences Building. What was particularly exceptional about his achievement was that he agreed, after several months of delicate negotiations by the Director of Development, that only his last name had to be used on the building. The money saved could be added to the fund to buy a bust of the donor to be placed in the foyer. The commonest honorary degree is D.D., or Doctor of Divinity, qualifying a minister to apply smelling salts to members of the congregation who faint during an overlong sermon.

Horizontal enrichment. (1) Addition of new learning opportunities at the student's present level of achievement rather than acceleration of the student's program. (2) Another form of horizontal enrichment is for the student to lie down and go to sleep, wearing headphones. Enrichment may also be accomplished by adding vitamins or increasing the student's allowance.

Hygiene. From the Greek *hygieinos*, healthful. A study of physical health, beginning in kindergarten with instruction in brushing teeth, combing hair, and lifting the toilet seat.[1] Other forms of hygiene are sex

[1] Something a little extra for boys.

hygiene, calling attention to the sex organs if they have been overlooked, and mental hygiene, which tries to keep the mind clean, especially during instruction in sex hygiene.

I. First person singular pronoun, used frequently by teachers and even more often by superintendents and principals. (2) Incomplete, a grade given when a student is prevented by illness from completing a course. Some teachers, who from years of experience have learned not to trust students, require X-rays and a blood sample. If the student does not complete the work by a certain date, the I is changed to an F. This is done very easily by drawing a line to the right of the top of the I and another line, slightly shorter, at the middle.

Identity. Finding out who you are. This is difficult for young children who do not have credit cards, a Social Security number, or even a driver's license. It is not enough, as it once was, simply to answer "Here" when the roll is called. True identity comes only when the student exclaims, "Oh, there I am!" after years of searching and, especially during adolescence, reflecting (i.e., looking for hours into a mirror). Teachers can help students discover their identity by assigning papers on such personal subjects as "An Analysis of My Analyst" and "The Last Time I Saw Dad." Some teachers, however, may still be trying to find themselves themselves.

Idiot savant. A mentally retarded person who in some area has above-average ability. Thus a student may be unable to add two and two, write a complete sentence, or tie his shoelaces and yet be a child prodigy at the piano. More frequently encountered, however, is the "idiot savant" who has an encyclopedic knowledge of history, literature, and philosophy but is always forgetting his umbrella or, if he has it, can't figure out how to open the thing. "Now let me see," he says, standing in a mud puddle while a drenching rain comes down. Ordinary idiots are locked up in a nice, dry asylum.

Independent work. Work performed by students with the minimum of supervision. At the college level it is called independent study, presumably because less work is involved. Permitting, even encouraging, students to do independent work is recognition of the ability of the students or the laziness of the teacher. Independent students rarely go near the teacher, or even the library.

Individual spelling demon. A word that a particular student always has trouble spelling. At least such a student is particular and wishes to spell correctly. A student's spelling demon may be "cat," which he is forever spelling "kat" or "catt." This same student has no trouble at all with "supercalifragilisticexpialidocius." The rule of "i before e except after c" may help the student if he can avoid words like "leisure," "counterfeit," "veil," "weigh," etc. Then there is the phonetic way of learning spelling, which once led a foreigner to spell "fish" "ghoti": "gh" as in "cough," "o" as in "women," and "ti" as in "nation."[1]

Individualized instruction. Instruction that is tailored to the needs and abilities of the individual student. If ideal conditions were to prevail, there would be a special curriculum for each student, perhaps a teacher for each student, and everyone would be happy but the taxpayer.

Infirmary. A place where students are kept when they have an infirmity. The best thing about being in the infirmary is that it is considered an Excused Absence. The worst thing is the food.

Information retrieval. Obtaining information from computers and other machines by pressing a button, spinning a dial, or passing one's hand in front of a photoelectric cell. Eventually information retrieval will take the place of books, teachers, and perhaps even students, certain machines placing information in other machines and still other machines retrieving it. Teachers and students will have nothing to do but twiddle their thumbs, and small machines (digital computers) will be available to do the twiddling.

In group. A group of persons who are on the inside, feel as if they belong, are "with it." The in group of teachers, for instance, call the principal by his first

[1] Some students memorize lists of Words Most Often Misspelled. They memorize them in their misspelled form, of course.

name. They may even slap him on the back and think they are getting away with it, at least until the next teaching assignments are made. In connection with the in group, it might be remarked that though there is an outhouse there is no such thing as an inhouse.[1] In group students study together, date together, and smoke pot together. They dislike anyone trying to get in, especially the police.

In loco parentis. A Latin expression meaning "in place of the parent," i.e., the teacher doing what the parent failed to do at home, such as giving the child a good thrashing. Some, who think the expression is Spanish, believe it refers to crazy parents, and they could be right.

Innovative. Anything different in the content or technique of education, the assumption being that anything different is better (if you are a liberal) or dangerous (if you are a conservative).

Input. What is put into a computer, in the hope that something more informative will come out. Teachers used to tell students, "You get out of a thing only what you put into it." But that was in the Good Old Days, when you could have bought IBM stock for ten dollars a share.

Intellectual maturation. Development of rational, conceptual, and logical powers, referred to by persons not in the field of Education as growing up.

Interaction of experience. A meaningful exchange between an individual and his environment. As Profes-

[1] There is, however, an inn.

sor Good says, "A boy, for example, does not learn from cutting himself with his jackknife unless he relates his purposes, a sharp blade, an object to be shaped, an unprotected finger" (*Dictionary of Education*, p. 295). Otherwise he just stands there crying, with the blood dripping, and shortly afterward proceeds to cut another finger. Ultimately he either (1) runs out of fingers, (2) learns to use a dull knife, (3) wears a leather glove, or (4) says to his father, "Here, you do this."[1]

Interdisciplinary. A fusion or confusion of two or more related fields of study, such as Economics and Religion or Art and Chemistry. The purpose of interdisciplinary studies is to know less about more, thereby achieving breadth. Paradoxically, the increase in disciplines leads to a decrease in discipline.

Interest-centered individualized reading approach. A technique in teaching reading skills that considers the child as an individual and tries to discover what he is interested in reading. This technique has not been widely enough used to permit a conclusive judgment regarding its effectiveness, but dropping *Silas Marner* from certain reading lists and replacing it with *Candy* has seemed to help.[2]

[1] The boy is learning. If his father also cuts himself, the boy will learn yet another important lesson: Older people are not necessarily any smarter.

[2] The interest-centered approach was discovered when a teacher said "textbook" but a student thought she said "sex book." From the expression on the student's face, the teacher could see that he was interested.

Intern. Formerly a medical term, now applied to a teacher going through a transitional stage before being entrusted with young minds. The intern is a little like someone who has a learner's permit but is not yet permitted to drive the car alone or at night. An intern observes the teaching methods of experienced teachers and in turn[1] is observed by an experienced teacher. If, after such observation, the intern still wishes to teach, there is probably nothing anyone can do about it. In this connection, the educational world seems to be borrowing more and more from the medical profession: such titles as "doctor" and "intern," psychiatric methods in counseling, etc. Eventually a principal's secretary may be called a nurse and his outer office, with his diplomas displayed on the wall, a waiting room. By that time, Edicare will see young people through college. Already a great many teachers, especially professors in large lecture courses, are experts in anesthesiology.

Interpersonal relations. Relations between two or more students, considered helpful in socialization, acculturization, group identity, behavior patterns, the development of attitudinal resources, and no telling (unless you are an educational psychologist) what other good things. Interpersonal relations are especially interesting when two students are on a date, the girl calling on all the attitudinal resources at her command, and sometimes for help.

[1] The original meaning and spelling.

Interview. A face-to-face meeting[1] of teacher and student, parent and teacher, principal and teacher, or counselor and student. One or the other, and sometimes both, will be nervous, and the thoughtful host will provide candy, cigarettes, and worry beads. The interviewer tries to ask searching questions without seeming too inquisitive, and the interviewee tries to appear calm while cracking his knuckles and wiping the sweat from his brow. An interview is not to be confused with a confrontation. In an interview neither party tries to make his point by opening a switchblade knife or cocking a revolver.

Introversion-extroversion test. A test to determine whether a person inclines to be reflective and introspective or more the social, gregarious type. The first, or introvert, should be guided toward a career as a hermit, while the second, or extrovert, should be advised to prepare for life work as a used-car salesman. Occasionally the test papers of an introvert and an extrovert are switched and there are serious consequences. The next time you see a timid, withdrawn used-car salesman, a copy of the *Rubáiyát* sticking out of his pocket, you can be pretty sure this is what happened.

[1] With two-faced people, this can be complicated.

Involvement. The state of being involved. Today students demand involvement in such matters as admissions, curriculum, and the hiring and firing of professors. Because of the many demands on their time, they have not as yet manifested any desire to become involved in fund raising, which they leave to the trustees. Inasmuch as students consider the trustees narrow-minded and incompetent, this reveals a generous, tolerant attitude.

IQ. Intelligence Quotient. The mental age (determined by an intelligence test) divided by the chronological age. Thus a child with a mental age of 12 and an actual age of 10 has an IQ of 1.2 (usually expressed as 120).[1] The norm, which is none too high, is 100. No matter how old the testee is, in computing the IQ a child is never supposed to be over 16 years of age, perhaps because the arithmetic gets too difficult for the average educational psychologist.[2]

Isolation. A student is said to be isolated when he is outside his peer group, looking in. He may also be a Peeping Tom.

[1] Imagine how a parent would feel if told, "Your child has an IQ of 1.2."
[2] It would be interesting to know the IQ of the average educational psychologist, wouldn't it?

Janitor. *Obs.* See "Custodian."

Judiciary. A student court before which offenders[1] are brought. Members of the Judiciary have the power to determine the guilt or innocence of their fellow students and to sentence the guilty to such penalties as a week's encampusment or an hour of sweeping walks. Serious infraction of rules, or infraction of serious rules, may involve expulsion, excommunication, or execution.[2] Such cases are referred to the Dean of Students, who refers them to the President, who refers them to the Board of Trustees. The trustees, who persist in the old-fashioned idea that college is a place for study, say, "Throw the book at them." If they are in a really bad mood, they mean the unabridged dictionary.

Jungle gym. An apparatus used for climbing activities. Grown-ups who hear students speak of this think they are referring to Jungle Jim, a character in Kipling. (See also Jungle Jane.) Actually the jungle gym is a maze consisting of vertical and horizontal ladders from which climbers may fall onto the cement strategically placed below by bone specialists.

[1] And not merely those with bad breath.
[2] Ex marks the spot.

Junior college. A high school with ashtrays. More popularly known as a "community college," a "two-year college," or almost anything not containing the word "junior." Some persons with a Ph.D. prefer to teach at such an institution, where they are looked up to with a certain amount (or degree) of awe. Many junior college students take what is known as a terminal program. This means that when they have had it they have had it, insofar as education is concerned. On graduation from a junior college a student is granted the degree of A.A., which means Associate in Arts and has nothing to do with efforts to stop drinking.

Junior high school. Between elementary school and high school, when students become adolescents and for the first time are not only curious about sex but able to do something about it. Male teachers in a junior high school are still slightly taller, heavier, and more muscular than their students, and need to be. The junior high school has been viewed tenderly by the poet who wrote the following lines:

> My heart leaps up when I behold
> The school where I was once enrolled,
> Where once I sat in study hall
> And studied little if at all,
> Where at the blackboard, chalk in hand,
> All I could do was grin and stand,
> Where I loved Susan, had it bad,
> While Susan loved another lad.
>
> My heart leaps up when I pass by
> Old Central Union Junior High.

It always gives me pleasure when
I think: They'll not get me again! [1]

Junior year abroad. A student spends the junior year in Paris, Munich, or Florence, after studying the language for two years in high school and two years in college. But he cannot understand it when he gets there, because everyone speaks too rapidly.[2] He also cannot speak it, because by the time he works out the correct form of the verb and the gender of the noun, everyone has left. However, by spending all of his time with other American students he finds language no problem.

Kindergarten. From the German *Kinder*, children, and *Garten*, garden. Apparently the Germans planted their children in rows, watered them frequently, and watched them grow until they were big enough to transplant in a *Schule*, school. In America, kindergarten is a place where children, usually age four to six, engage in organized play activities. These activities permit self-expression with clay, paint, and blocks. Throwing these articles at each other has a

[1] The first line of this poem was stolen from Wordsworth, a practice the author learned in high school and perfected in college.

[2] The natives are restless.

socializing tendency. Children are brought close together, to get within range, and teachers are brought running.

Kindergarten visiting program. A program for visits to kindergarten by children who plan to attend kindergarten the next year. Visitors are classified as t.t. and n.t.t.[1] One result of this program is that when next year arrives and these children are ready to go to kindergarten, some of them will have to be dragged there, screaming.

Laboratory. A place where scientific experiments are carried out. In chemistry lab, if the wrong chemicals are mixed the student may be carried out also. The scope of laboratory work is enormous, ranging from the microscope to the telescope and, in undersea laboratories, the periscope. The pre-medical student works in a laboratory with a beaker and a Bunsen burner and dreams of medical school, where he will have the latest X-ray equipment and his own cadaver.

Laterality. Having to do with reading from side to side, preferably left to right. Students unable to do this have a reading problem. One solution is to send

[1] Toilet-trained and not toilet-trained. Young visitors sit around and watch, and it is while they are sitting that you can't be sure.

them to Japan, where they read from top to bottom. This could become a new kind of cultural exchange, such students being exchanged for Japanese students who are having a verticality problem.[1]

Liberal education. Some parents believe there should be equal time for conservative education, featuring Discipline 243 a, b, Elementary and Advanced Thrift, and Riot Control, a prerequisite for Law (first semester) and Order (second semester).

Library. A place where the books a student desperately needs are either lost or charged out by a student who has gone home for two weeks. Some books are on General Reserve, while others are on General Grant, General Eisenhower, etc. The library can best be summed up in the following immortal lines:

> Here is where people,
> One frequently finds,
> Lower their voices
> And raise their minds.

Linoleum cut. A way of making illustrations in Art class. Linoleum cuts can be made with linoleum cut from the floor, as long as the linoleum lasts. It may then be necessary to make woodcuts.[2] One advantage of woodcuts is that, while at work, the student can mutter, "Who cuts wood like a woodcut would if a woodcut could cut wood?" This has a nice beat. Besides, it bothers others students in the class less than whistling.

[1] Laterality also involves the dominance of one hand, eye, or foot over the other. If you are left-handed, just think of the difficulties of a student who is also left-footed, left-eyed, and very likely left behind.

[2] As a last resort, the student can cut classes.

69

Load. The number of hours a college professor spends in the classroom each week. These are sometimes called "contact hours," though physical contact between professor and student is not encouraged. Nine or more hours a week is considered a heavy load, but persons not in the teaching profession and not knowing about preparation, committee work, correcting papers, departmental intrigue, and filling out applications for grants and fellowships think a nine-hour week (as compared with their forty) is scandalous. Professors with a nine-hour load are always on the lookout for a position with a six-hour load, and those with a six-hour load are always looking for a position with a three-hour load. The ideal position involves no teaching whatsoever and is called a Distinguished Professorship. It draws the top salary, since a professor who is able to avoid teaching completely is either very experienced or a Scholar of International Renown whose mere presence Graces the Campus.

Locker. A metal cabinet that may be locked to protect clothing, books, pornographic literature, marijuana, and other items of real or sentimental value. Lock-picking is not taught as a course but must be picked up by students who forget their combination. In some school somewhere there must be a student named Davy Jones who takes a ribbing about Davy Jones's locker. He probably doesn't know that Davy Jones is a corruption of Duppy Jones, and "duppy" is a word used in the West Indies for a ghost or malevolent spirit. It is true that when he opens his locker, with those sweat socks and old tennis shoes inside, a malevolent spirit, or smell, creeps out.

Machine shop. A room equipped with machinery for learning how to make and repair things. The first thing the student learns how to repair is the machinery, which breaks down frequently enough to provide almost continuous instruction. More advanced work includes learning how to remove the grease from under the fingernails. In time the student can make useful items, such as a collapsible chair. (Eventually he may be able to make a chair that doesn't collapse.) Shop training is increasingly important to the home craftsman, now that a carpenter is likely to charge around ten dollars an hour and a plumber is almost as reluctant as a doctor to make a house call. The ability to use a hammer, a screwdriver, and a pipe wrench is essential in our Do-It-Yourself Society, a society in which if you ask a painter to touch up a few spots he missed, he is likely to hand you the brush and can of paint and say, "Do it yourself." If the school bonds fail to pass, even a teacher may need to know how to repair a leak in the roof or track down a short in the lighting system, while students stand around hoping to see an electrocution.

Major. Can be either a field of concentration or an Army officer of field grade. The way you can tell the two majors apart is that when a college girl tells a friend, "I'm taking an interesting major," she is referring to her field of concentration. If she says, "I'm being taken by an interesting major," she is still referring to her field of concentration, but he is an officer in the ROTC unit.[1]

Mal. (1) Abbreviation for physically maladjusted, used in P.E. classes. Preferable to "stum" for "stumble-bum." A student can also be described as psychologically maladjusted if he doesn't like his roommate, courses, teachers, or parents, and has been seen beating a dog. Anyone who becomes a buddy of such a person would appear to be a little out of adjustment himself. (2) Nickname for a boy named Malcolm.

Manual proficiency. Ability to use the hands, envied by students who are good in subjects like literature and philosophy but have no chance of ever becoming a truck driver or a masseur and will have to settle for a career in law, politics, or even teaching.

Margin. (1) In English composition, the space between the writing and the edge of the paper. English teachers are onto the fact that the wider the margins—top, bottom, left, and right—the fewer words it takes to complete an assigned four-page paper. (2) In finance, what a purchaser of stocks buys on if he wants to risk losing his shirt.[2]

[1] They are probably going to the Military Ball, which soldiers with fixed (hastily repaired) bayonets will protect from a menacing crowd of pacifists, armed with shotguns and Molotov cocktails.

[2] Something understood, let us hope, by the Finance Committee of a Board of Trustees.

PHO- NET' IC

Meaning attack. Figuring out the meaning of a word by the context in which the word is found rather than attacking the word itself. Thus in the sentence, "The rat ate the cheese," the word "cheese," as the teacher wisely points out, "must be something edible, don't you think?" "What is edible?" a student asks, and the teacher, who has been attacking, is on the defensive. Meaning attack is slower than looking up a word in the dictionary, but there is something more sporting about it.

Meaningful. Having meaning. Used as often as possible by teachers and, especially, administrators. See "Relevance."

Mental block. The inability to think. Likely to occur to a student when suddenly called upon in class, or

73

to a teacher when called into the principal's office.
A mental block is somewhat more serious than a
stumbling block, because psychiatrists' fees are
higher than bone surgeons'.

Modular scheduling. Scheduling of classes by modules,
say ten-minute periods that can be put together in
various combinations for the sake of flexibility. Excellent for high-school students with a ten-minute
attention span. Also guaranteed to drive the average
teacher to drink. The above-average teacher will
be drinking already. By means of modules, classes
can be made up into almost any length, from ten
minutes (one module) to four hours (twenty-four
modules), and no one knows what class is meeting
when or for how long except by consulting a chart.
Finding a given class on the chart takes approxi-

mately one module. Students especially enjoy free modules, when there is nothing to do but sit around and wait for the next module.[1]

Monitor. From the Latin *monere*, to warn, to remind. A monitor is a student who is assigned to perform special duties. Since it is good for every student to be some sort of monitor to give him a sense of

responsibility, and since some teachers may have difficulty thinking up a monitorship for everyone, a few suggestions are offered herewith:[2]

1. Time monitor, responsible for watching the clock and telling everyone what time it is.

2. Closet monitor. If it is a very large closet, this may be divided into upper-shelf monitor and lower-shelf monitor.

[1] "Module," which comes from the Latin *modulus*, a small measure, is not to be confused with "nodule," which comes from the Latin *nodulus*, a little lump. It is related to "model" and "mode," and suggests revising W. S. Gilbert's famous line to read "I am the very module of a module modern principal."

[2] Many of these will be found in Katherine C. La Mancusa's *We Do Not Throw Books at the Teacher*, pp. 41–43. I never did find out what the students *do* throw at the teacher.

3. Wastebasket monitor, responsible for picking up objects thrown at the wastebasket that missed.

4. Errand monitor, responsible for seeing that anyone sent on an errand comes back.

5. Phonograph needle monitor, capable of finding a needle in a haystack.

6. Plant monitor, responsible for watering, with demerits for running over.

7. Wall monitor. Preferably a student who is wall-eyed.

8. Ceiling monitor, permitted to lie flat on his back in pursuit of his duties.

9. Door monitor. If specialization is desired, open-door and closed-door monitor.

10. Pencil monitor, the only monitor who can say, "Get the lead out" without offense.

11. Pencil sharpener monitor. Works hand in glove (a safety precaution) with finger-in-pencil-sharpener monitor.

12. Science table monitor. Carries fire extinguisher at all times.

13. Library table monitor. Must perfect his "Sh-h-h-h!"

14. Bookmark monitor, responsible for objects left in books that are irreparably squashed.

15. Art table monitor, responsible for keeping the detachable figleaf on nude statues.

16. Milk monitor. Preferably of Chinese ethnic origin, with a name like Lo Fat.

17. Cracker monitor. "Crumby" to his friends.

18. Light monitor. Charged, and sometimes highly charged, with turning light on and off. An assignment for a student with a high IQ.

19. Blackboard monitor. "Keep it clean," he is instructed.

20. Chalk monitor, responsible for maintaining classroom morale when chalk squeaks.

21. Visitor monitor, responsible for warning, "Somebody's coming!"

22. Roll monitor, responsible for taking the roll, and not to be confused with the roll monitor who sees that no one has his roll taken from him at lunch.

23. Monitor monitor, also known as undercover agent, 007, quisling, and teacher's pet.

For a class of not more than twenty-three students, this list, though only a sampling, should suffice.[1]

Mononucleosis. The favorite disease of students. It is painless, never fatal, and requires six months off for rest. In medical terms, mononucleosis is characterized by the presence of an excessive number of mononuclears.

Motivation. The reason for doing something difficult or distasteful, such as reading *The Faerie Queene*,

[1] Other monitors, however, are *The Christian Science Monitor* and the ironclad that defeated the *Merrimac*.

finding a square root,[1] dissecting a frog, or pretending to like the teacher. Students may be motivated by promise of a motor scooter if they get good grades or fear of having their allowance cut if they get poor grades. Teachers may be motivated by the desire to move up to a more powerful and higher paying position, such as that of vice-principal.

Motor-perceptual skills. Skills developed in training a student to be an automobile mechanic. At the end of the course a student can listen to a motor, if he is really perceptual, and tell whether it needs a new thingamabob and, more important, what it will cost to install one. A student without motor-perceptual skills can tell that a motor is missing, but only by looking where it is supposed to be.

Muller-Schumann paradigm of associative inhibition. This Muller is not the same as the Müller, known as Umlaut Müller, of the Müller-Walle method of teaching lip reading.[2] The Muller-Schumann theory is that when an association has been formed between two items, it is more difficult to form an association between either of these two items and a third item. When two items such as a husband and wife have formed an association for many years, and then the husband takes up with another woman, twenty years younger and thirty pounds lighter than his wife, difficulties of forming a new association may include a

[1] Most roots are round.
[2] Reading the lips with the lips instead of the fingers is known as kissing. Unlike artificial respiration, there is nothing artificial about it, and both parties are soon breathing heavily.

messy divorce, alimony, and restricted visits from the children. The nasty truth could be, of course, that there was something brewing between Mrs. Muller and Dr. Schumann.

Multiple choice. A type of question that gives a choice of several answers, one of which is right. Given a choice of (a), (b), or (c), the student who merely guesses will, according to the law of averages, pick the correct answer about a third of the time. This will give him a grade of around 33, which is only 27 below passing. On the other hand, on a true-false test he may make as high as 50 just by flipping a coin, though such a student, flip though he may be, often doesn't have a coin.

Nervous belching. Known in Latin, in which it sounds better, as *eructatio nervosa*. A child who belches may not be trying to annoy the teacher or gain the attention and admiration of his peers. If it is true *eructatio nervosa*, he simply cannot help it, and slapping him on the back or stuffing a handkerchief into his mouth will do no good. He can be told to go out and get a drink of water, in the hope that he won't come back, or he can be sent to the school nurse, with a note saying simply "N.B.," which can be taken as either "Nervous belching" or "Nota bene." The situation becomes more embarrassing if the teacher, and not a student, suffers an attack of *eructatio nervosa*, or if the thing is contagious, and soon everyone in the class is belching in unison, led by the teacher's deeper, more resonant *eructatio*.[1]

New math. Different from ye olde math, the idea being to keep students who have a mental block against mathematics from knowing they are working on a math problem until it is solved. By calling multiplication "stretching" and division "shrinking," the teacher can make the student think he is in an easy course in P.E. or Art. Two and two are still four, but in the new math the solution, when it comes, has philosophical overtones. Students have described solution of a mathematics problem by the new method as a revelation or mystical experience, with sensations comparable to those they get from LSD. Once caught by the new math, some students are unable to kick it until they find themselves stuck for life as computer programmers. New teachers are better at new math than old teachers, since they have nothing to unlearn.[2]

Nonresident tuition. A fee paid by a university student who lives in another state. The antonym for nonresident tuition is resident nontuition.[3] Nonresident tui-

[1] Students usually snicker when they come across the name of Sir Toby Belch, in *Twelfth Night*. This is about what Shakespeare expected. When I was in high school, the principal's name was Mr. Belcher, and that got some laughs too.

[2] There is also new grammar, which has had some tragic consequences. See Browning's "A Grammarian's Funeral."

[3] Also known as intuition.

tion is a small sum, but to avoid paying it families will give up their jobs, sell their homes, and move to another state. "It's the principle of the thing," they say, and that is about as good an explanation as you are likely to get.

Norm. A national average used in tests, especially the Iowa Test, a test to discover how much the average student knows about Iowa. Once the norm is determined, a student can be found to be either so much above the norm or so much below the norm. The student may, indeed, be exactly on the norm, but this is frowned upon. Such a student would present no challenge. If there were many like him, the suicide rate among educational psychologists would be even higher than it is today.

Normal school. An institution for the education of teachers, now generally known as a teachers college[1] or a school of education. The term "Normal" was dropped when other institutions objected to the implication that they were not. Typical courses at such an institution are "The Historical, Sociological, and Philosophical Foundations of Education" (Prerequisite: "Classroom Control by the Use of Mace"), "Methodology" (limited to Methodists), and "Practicum in Educational Administration" (for those interested in learning what a practicum is).

[1] Whether it should be "teachers college," "teacher's college," or "teachers' college" has led to considerable bitterness and establishment of three schools of thought. A school of thought has no buildings or faculty.

81

Nursery school. (1) A school to train nurserymen. (2) A place where small children are kept instead of hiring a baby sitter. Education in a nursery school concentrates on such basic principles as: (a) Modeling clay is not to eat; (b) Building blocks are not to throw; (c) If you don't stop screaming we'll chain you to the plumbing. Nursery-school teachers have had courses in "Personality Development," "Children

in Contemporary Cultures," and "Language and Cognition in Children," and *should* be able to cope with any situation. After all, they are only teaching until they can find a husband who agrees that childless marriages are best.[1]

[1] Or simply until they can find a husband. With each passing year their requirements are fewer.

Off-campus living. Students living in apartments and without supervision. To some, off-campus living has much the same quality as off-color joking. Older people think the worst, and they are usually right.

Old grad. A graduate who is not necessarily old but, to those still in college, seems so. He suffers from a bad case of nostalgia, which causes him to talk incessantly about the Good Old Days and to get a lump in his throat at the mention of professors like Good Old Hinshaw, Good Old Grigsby, and Good Old Norcross, all of whom he hated when he got D's in their courses. In his weakened condition, he may be persuaded to give a hundred dollars to the Building Fund, but will recover quickly enough to stop payment on the check.[1]

One-way vision observation. A technique, using a special screen or mirror, which permits the observer to watch the subject without the subject's knowing it. Though it is now used chiefly in studies of infant and child behavior, there is no reason why it cannot be more widely employed. Consider its usefulness to a principal, checking up on a new teacher, or to a

---

[1] There must be something wrong with his eyes, too, because he constantly views with alarm.

superintendent, checking up on a new principal. Consider how helpful it would be, with a one-way viewer installed in the teacher's lounge, to members of the American Legion who have heard that certain teachers are encouraging others to sign their loyalty oath with their fingers crossed.[1] To revise Proverbs XXIX, 18 ever so slightly: "Where there is no one-way vision, the peepers perish."

Oral examination. (1) Examination by a nose-and-throat specialist. (2) Examination by means of the spoken word. The oral examination is a boon to students who have trouble with spelling but a little hard on stutterers. It is difficult to crib on an oral examination but easy to sling the bull, milk the cow, and wean the calf, i.e., digress. There is always the chance that the instructor will forget what the question was.

Output. What comes out of a computer. (See "Input," above.) The mouse that came out of the computer in Schenectady on September 26, 1967, is reported to have climbed in there by himself and was not a result of programming.

[1] Not easy to do. Try it sometime.

Overt behavior. What a student does out in the open, as contrasted with what he does behind the teacher's back. What he does behind the teacher's back is likely to be more revealing of the student's attitudinal responses, and the teacher who wishes to know the worst is advised to turn around suddenly.[1]

Parietal. Pertaining to life within the walls or buildings of a college, from the Latin *paries, -ietis*, a wall. This does not mean, however, such life within the walls as creatures that come out of the woodwork, though this may be the belief of students with regard to certain professors. An institution bears a parietal relationship to its students when it regulates their lives and treats them like children, whereas students wish to be treated like adults, not realizing how much worse adults are treated. Students resent being thought immature, and therefore demonstrate their

[1] Many a teacher has exclaimed, "How I wish I had eyes in the back of my head!" With the work now being done with genes, such a teacher may yet be developed.

maturity by staying out all night, driving recklessly, being sexually promiscuous, shouting obscenities, and locking themselves in the Dean's office. One way they escape the parietal domination of the college is to live off-campus, or outside the walls, where they can look back wistfully at dormitory life, with no cooking of meals, scrubbing of floors, or dealing with a landlady who is always threatening to cancel the lease.

Pass-Fail. Instead of a letter grade, a simple Pass or Fail may be given. This removes one of the more sordid reasons for striving to excel and pressing onward toward excellence. The Pass-Fail grading system permits the student to put off competing with others until after graduation. Not having developed the competitive spirit, he may be a failure in everything he tries until, at last, someone suggests a career in teaching.

Patrol. An organization of students who assist other students in complying with safety regulations, such as looking both ways at once while crossing the crosswalk in front of the school. Members of the patrol may occasionally wave a student into the path of an oncoming truck, but this is quite unintentional. Patrol members are rarely accused of police brutality.[1]

Peephole method. A method for observing eye movements by looking through a small hole in a card while the subject reads what is written on the other side of the card. This may be an instance of pedagogical

[1] Since they are on duty only during the day, it would be silly to equip them with nightsticks.

voyeurism,[1] or the teacher may be playing oculist. At any rate, anyone who peeps at eye movements through a small hole all day long is worth whatever he is paid.

Peer group. Not to be confused with (1) members of the House of Lords or (2) a group of longshoremen. In education, a peer group is a group of students of about the same age and ability who, also being about the same height, can peer at each other on equal footing. In this sense the word "peer" goes back to the Latin *par*, meaning equal. A student who is peerless is therefore someone without an equal, and it would be difficult to fit him into any class in school. He would probably have to be given independent study. See Peer Gynt, a Norwegian dropout who got most of his education from trolls, none of whom was certificated.

Pep assembly. Sometimes called a pep rally. "Pep" is an abbreviation of "pepper," and a pep assembly should be spicier than it is. It is a gathering of students for the purpose of creating mass hysteria just before the Big Game. (Big game in this instance is not what is hunted in Africa but an athletic contest between rival schools.) Cheerleaders in very short skirts jump up and down and shake pompons.[2] Other scantily clad

[1] Made more titillating when the hole is shaped like a tiny keyhole.

[2] A pompon is a tuft of some sort, while a pompom, which is what most people call it, is an automatic cannon, so named from the sound it makes. Cheerleaders are not likely to jump up and down waving pompoms unless they are leading a well-armed group of militants.

girls twirl batons in an unnecessary effort to call attention to themselves. There are speeches, yells, and songs, the success of a pep assembly being judged by the volume of noise. From the standpoint of students, the ideal pep assembly meets at what would normally be a regular class hour.

Percentile. A point on a scale of test scores which a certain percentage of scores are above. For instance, a score in the 34th percentile means that 66 percent of the scores are higher, which should not give the taker of the test any great sense of satisfaction. It helps, though, to realize that 33 percent are lower. This is counting percentiles from the bottom. Some count percentiles from the top, in which case the above figures would be reversed and everyone would be confused, which is normal. In education almost everything that falls, falls into one percentile or another, except for those things that fall onto the floor or into the wastebasket. The word "percent" comes from the Latin *per centum*, per hundred. If this is too difficult, remember that there are one hundred cents in a dollar, one hundred years in a century, and one hundred feet (more or less) on a centipede.[1] Gradually it begins to dawn on you, even if you are not mathematically inclined.

Permissiveness. A term used by parents to describe the activities of teachers who think they are being understanding, creative, and up-to-date.

[1] Or in a centipede if the centipede has eaten another centipede.

Pes planus. Flatfoot. If a teacher wishes to tell some-one, within the student's hearing, that the student has this condition, she can say, "Joe has *pes planus.*" Joe won't know what is being said about him, but he may think it is something worse.

Phi Beta Kappa. The oldest Greek-letter society, less given to drinking and wild parties than most fraternities. Members, called Phi Bates, can be recognized by their peculiar two-fingered handshake and by their

even more peculiar key, which is incapable of un-locking anything. The key is dangled from a watch chain, from a charm bracelet, or, by the more ostentatious, from the nose.

Phonics. A method of teaching reading by means of the analysis of sounds. The usefulness of this method is at once apparent when you consider the spelling and pronunciation of such words as "though," "tough," "through," and "cough."

Phonic strip. Not a comic (funny) strip or a burlesque act, but a list of phonograms placed on a card and used for drill in phonic recognition. Unlike a strip-tease, in which more and more is revealed slowly, with a phonic strip somewhat less is revealed more and more quickly.

Pie chart. (1) A chart used by the baker in the school cafeteria. (2) A circular graph, the segments looking like pieces of pie, used to indicate how the budget is chopped up and what a small slice is left for teachers' salaries compared with Miscellaneous.

Placement service. (1) A term used in tennis. (2) A service offered by an educational institution to old-fashioned students who wish employment. Representatives seeking intelligent, ambitious, clean-cut young men[1] come from private industry and from the Armed Services. Even when these representatives are not from the Army or Air Force, they are called recruiters, and if they represent a company that is part of the Military-Industrial Complex, making a war-related product such as processed cheese or toothbrushes, they are ringed by pickets and shouted down during interviews. Recruiters from industry are no longer able to tempt the better students with promises of a gray flannel suit, an attaché case, and membership in the country club, but must compete with the Peace Corps in offering opportunities for learning Swahili and getting malaria and/or dysentery. Some students, however, still are so crass and unidealistic as to have visions of a home and fam-

[1] Harder and harder to find, much less to interest.

ily, and even a savings account with which to pay for the education of their children instead of expecting a government handout. Such students make furtive appointments in off-campus motels, hoping no one sees them sign up with Chase Manhattan or Colgate Palmolive. It could make things pretty unpleasant for them during the last months before graduation. If a student keeps his hat on during the interview, it is because he is unwilling to make the supreme sacrifice, just yet, and cut his hair. Since he is thinking of going into business, he does, however, wear a business suit, which he has rented or perhaps borrowed from a friend of the family.[1] The Placement Director, by the way, has been hymned in these touching lines:

> Who weeps not for the placement lad
> Must have a heart of stone.
> He gets jobs for the college grad
> That pay more than his own.

Platoon plan. A plan whereby students are divided into two groups, or platoons, one doing classroom work while the other engages in such applied activities as swinging on the monkey bars. The two platoons alternate, thus keeping all facilities in continuous use. This makes the taxpayer happy and keeps the principal under constant tension. It would help if each platoon had a sergeant to bark out orders and keep the students in line.

[1] He may even wear a dark business suit, though this may suggest that he is willing to go into some dark, or after-dark, business, such as the CIA.

Potential. Untapped power; what is possible but not probable. Good teaching is supposed to draw out the student's potential, but it usually comes out hard, like molasses. Students who do not live up to their potential receive comments on their papers and examinations such as "This is not your best work" and "You can do better." These remarks are meant to be encouraging, but the student who did his best and still got a D is not cheered up. If his parents helped him with the paper, the whole family is furious.

Practice teaching. Teaching by a student teacher who is learning by doing. On-the-job training of teachers at the expense of students. A practice teacher usually teaches under the supervision of an experienced teacher who sits in the back of the classroom and makes faces. At the end of the class period the practice teacher asks, "How did I do?" An experienced teacher may now and then drop a few crumbs of praise along with the criticism, but the world is still waiting for one to come out with the honest truth: "You are a better teacher right now than I ever was."[1]

Prep school. Abbreviation for "preparatory school," a private school that prepares students for life's crises, such as not getting into the college of their choice. Usually a prep school preps for the institution to which the boy's father and grandfather went, and if the father is a big donor or, even better, both a big donor and a member of the Board of Trustees, the task is made somewhat easier. Some students are sent to a prep school not so much to help them get into

[1] If practice really makes perfect, teachers should be better than they are.

college as to get them away from home or out of trouble. They wear a blazer and a school tie so that they are easy to identify when they get into trouble again.

Pre-registration. Registration for courses well in advance, perhaps registering in the spring for courses in the fall. This affords ample time for students to change their minds and to take none of the courses for which they pre-registered. By making additional paperwork, pre-registration helps justify an overstaffed registrar's office.

Prerequisite. A course required to be taken before the student is eligible to take another course. Thus, Introductory French is a prerequisite for Intermediate French, and Intermediate French is a prerequisite for Advanced French. An intriguing possibility would be to require the student to start with Advanced and wind up with Introductory, in this way getting the hardest part over first and actually being able to enjoy Introductory.[1]

Pretest. A test given before a test in order to test the test and the testee. A pretext, however, is not a textbook used to prepare for another textbook.

Principal. Not to be confused with "principle," or with a person with principles. A principal (see the Latin *princeps*, from which we derive "prince") is the leader, the chief, the one who has controlling authority over subordinates in a school, and he never forgets this for a minute. As the head man, he has the power

[1] Usually there is no prerequisite for Philosophy, the Introductory and the Advanced being equally confusing.

to lop off heads, make heads roll, etc., and is therefore known, in a private school, as the Headmaster.[1]

Problem-oriented curriculum. In this type of curriculum the student learns by solving problems, for instance how to open your locker when you have forgotten the combination, how to smooth the pages of a library book you left out in the rain, and how to pass a note to a friend across the room without being seen. Teachers must be able to solve problems as quickly as students if they are to maintain any self-respect. An advantage of the problem-solving curriculum is that everything is a game. Instead of saying, "Now I understand," the student says, "I've won!"

Problem solving. Solving problems.

Programmed instruction. Instruction put together in packages for convenience of handling. The idea is to learn little by little, to avoid brain strain. Sometimes a student and a machine are put together in the same package; for instance, in a typing course, a student and a typewriter. They are kept together until either the student types sixty words a minute or the typewriter needs to be traded in for a new model. In programmed instruction everything proceeds according to plan, and the teacher who lacks originality, ingenuity, and rapport with students has nothing to worry about.[2]

---

[1] A woman principal is more inclined than a man principal to be concerned about small details. For her, each hour consists of sixty minutiae.

[2] Such a teacher gets off to a good start by cheerily asking, "Well, what's the program for today?"

Progressive education. Educating in a way that is different, assuming that anything that is different is better. Progressive education, beginning with Dewey (not the admiral but the other one), became progressively more progressive until it was found progressive (i.e., different) to be unprogressive. In progressive education the child is treated like an

adult, and vice versa. The adult, not being able to understand the character-building values of commotion in the classroom, is told to mind his own business and keep on paying taxes and voting for school bonds.

PTA. Parent-Teacher Association, formed for the purpose of getting parents out of the home and making teachers give up their free evenings. An active PTA group is one that holds more meetings than necessary. If the meetings are also longer than necessary, the local PTA is considered highly successful and commended by the national organization. It has been found that attendance by parents is best when the program involves a play, orchestra concert, or glee club sing in which their children perform. Parents keep their eyes riveted on their offspring, hoping they will not forget their lines, drop their music, or faint. While other children are performing, they pay polite attention, trying their best to hide the bored look and the sneer. Some parents who belong to the association visit their children's school only once a year, on Back-to-School Night, to discover what the teacher is really like whom their child has described as "an old witch." (She is an old witch.) The greatest honor awarded by the PTA is a Life Membership, a sure means of arousing jealousy on the part of those not receiving it.[1]

Public-address system. A device for amplifying sounds, usually called a PA. It enables a teacher in a large classroom or a speaker in an auditorium to interrupt the sleep of students in the back row. Announcements over the PA intercom bring the voice of the principal and sometimes the superintendent even into the lavatories, and everyone feels that there is Someone who cares.

Public relations coordinator. A member of the administrative staff, often someone with newspaper experience (perhaps a paper route), who tries to get favorable treatment by the news media. The PR

[1] There are two schools of thought about the PTA. One holds that there should be a hyphen in Parent-Teacher Association, while the other maintains that this is unnecessary. Without the hyphen, of course, a Parent Teacher could be a teacher who is a parent and is teaching to pick up enough extra money to pay the baby sitter.

coordinator is frequently a person who had hoped for a career as a writer but could never learn to type.

Publish-or-perish syndrome. The requirement at most colleges and universities that a professor publish something—anything—to be promoted or even to hold his job. The alternative to publishing (perishing) is so terrifying that professors break out in a cold sweat when they think of it. To achieve maximum benefits, a professor should publish articles and books which are filed away (unread) by fellow professors in the same field. Publication of a popular work with a wide readership is damaging. This, however, is highly unlikely, since most professors write in a manner that guarantees a limited readership.[1]

Q-sort. A method of testing personality by sorting into different piles cards with adjectives descriptive of his personality. Thus a subject may be asked to place in "most descriptive," "descriptive," and "not descriptive" piles a series of cards containing such words as "friendly," "aloof," "hostile," "brilliant," "average mentality," "stupid," etc. Given this opportunity to

[1] A prolific scholar is not a person with unusual procreative powers but a professor with a long bibliography.

describe himself, the subject will do about as you would under similar circumstances unless he is so brilliant as to choose an adjective like "stupid."

Qualitative. The opposite of quantitative. Teaching is judged qualitatively and teachers' salaries are judged quantitatively. Any connection between the two is purely coincidental.

Quarter. (1) Twenty-five cents. (2) One fourth of a school year, in colleges on the quarter system. The chief advantage of the quarter system is that courses are finished before the beginning of the Christmas vacation, and students can enjoy their vacation without feeling guilty about papers they should be writing or examinations they should be studying for. On the other hand, the semester system gives professors enough time to learn the names of some of their students before the new semester begins. The quarter versus the semester system ranks third among topics for erudite discussion at the faculty club, being outranked only by the salary scale and the weather.[1]

Queen of the sciences. A phrase referring to mathematics, thought to have been coined by a mathematician. A teacher who is known as "a prince of a fellow" can be in any field and is probably in another school and known only casually.[2]

[1] When two faculty members do not speak to each other, they may have had a bitter, name-calling argument over the quarter system. Then again, they may be in different departments.

[2] "Queen of the night," interestingly enough, is a tropical American climbing cactus, *Selenicereus grandiflorus*.

Queen of the Sciences

Questionnaire. A list of questions, for instance about cafeteria food or the library fine system,[1] with a space for the response to each question. Large spaces are left for questions calling for "Yes" or "No," and small spaces are left for questions such as "What improvements do you think could be made in the selection of textbooks?"

[1] "Fine," say some.

Quiz. A short test, often giving rise to a quizzical look on the faces of students.

Quotient. You cannot understand "quotient" without understanding "achievement quotient," "altitude (*sic*) quotient," "developmental quotient," "group intelligence quotient," "memory quotient," "motor quotient," "personality quotient," "reading quotient," "social quotient," etc. Since this is manifestly impos-. sible, no attempt at definition will be made.

R.A. (1) Regular Army. (2) Initials of the author. (3) Resident Assistant. An older student, at any rate old enough to know better, who lives in the dormitory and is someone for the students to go to when they are in trouble. Girl students are not in trouble as often as they were before the Pill. The R.A. knows the rules, such as "Sign in before signing out," "Do not charge long-distance calls to the Dean of Students,"

and "No smoking pot before breakfast." He also knows, if he is really knowledgeable, that knowing the rules is not the same as enforcing them, and it is easier to fool the Dean, whom you see maybe once a week, than the students, whom you see every day, morning till night. Actually the R.A. doesn't live from day to day but from emergency to emergency.[1]

Reading index. A means of indicating whether a student is reading up to capacity. The interesting thing about this is that the reading index was invented, according to one source, by a scholar named Marion Monroe. It is our theory that the inventor was actually Marilyn Monroe, and her method was to walk past a young man who was reading a book and note how long it took him to look up. The ordinary student would be reading up to capacity if he looked up the moment Marilyn appeared in his line of vision. A reader so engrossed in a textbook that he did not look up at all would soon be on his way to the counseling center.[2]

Reading period. Also known as "period of independent study." During this period college students have time to catch up on such classics as *Valley of the Dolls, Lady Chatterley's Lover,* and *Fanny Hill.* Some professors, missing the whole point of the reading period, spoil everything by assigning a paper.

[1] If you call that living.

[2] Of course the reading index might refer to the index finger, used by slow readers to point out each word, meanwhile framing the word on the lips, and by others to find something in the index. If the book has no index, page references may be tattooed on the index finger.

Realia. Tangible objects or specimens, such as the articles found in a boy's pockets or in his desk. It may be hard to believe your eyes, and you may say, "Why, those are unrealia!" If it doesn't move, it is probably only asleep.

Recess. In an elementary school, a short period between classes that seems shorter than it really is. Students relax from the rigors of the classroom by engaging

in such wholesome activities as hair pulling (girls) and fisticuffs (boys).[1] Occasionally they throw stones at windows, the sound of breaking glass relieving psychological tensions. Teachers assigned the task of supervising recess activities are advised to wear crash helmets. One teacher, told that she would avoid trouble if she "looked the other way," was seriously hurt by a flying Coke bottle.[2]

Recommendation. A written statement by a teacher or counselor, regarding the qualifications of a student, that should be discounted about 40 percent. If it has been shown to the student, it should be discounted

[1] Now that hair is worn shoulder length by both sexes, hair pulling is popular with boys too. (The author, as may be suspected, prefers leg pulling.)

[2] She was hit in the back of the head.

80 percent. The recommendation may be for a job, such as working in a service station, when stress should be laid on such qualities as high ideals, intellectual curiosity, and ability to do research. Or it may be an application to a graduate school, in which case it is well to emphasize popularity, physical agility, and neatness ("I have never known him to have dirt under his fingernails"). To be asked to write a recommendation is flattering, since it means that you are the kind of person who sees only good in people and has an unlimited supply of time and postage stamps.

Recruitment. Recruiting teachers is somewhat different from recruiting soldiers. Prospective teachers are not appealed to on the basis of anything so emotional as service to one's country, but rather promises of a good starting salary, annual increases, group insurance, faculty billiard and bowling facilities, long vacations, and attractive retirement benefits. All of these inducements are usually necessary to overcome the prospective teacher's innate dislike for young people.[1]

Relevance. Being relevant. Used as often as possible by teachers and administrators. See "Meaningful." Currently very current, but like last year's "dichotomy" may be *obs.* by the time this book is published. "Relevance" will be found, interestingly enough, in the following lines written by an educator:

[1] Eventually, if not enough college graduates volunteer to go into teaching, it may be necessary to institute the draft. Conscientious objectors to teaching and persons in such critical occupations as military service may be granted deferment.

"Prestigious" I am quick to use,
  "In depth" I say with ease.
I toss off "ecumenical"
  As well as "expertise."

"Involvement" and "commitment" both
  I sprinkle through my talk.
Not even, friends, at "relevance"
  Am I inclined to balk.

So let me join your little group.
  How happy you will be
To hear me speak of "dialogue"
  And "serendipity."

You'll find me really quite reliable.
I use "charisma" too, and "viable."

Report card. A card or piece of paper on which a report is made concerning a student's grades. The student is supposed to return the card with the signature of one parent. A student who is no good at anything else may discover a special talent for forgery.

Requirement. A subject or course a student is required to take in order to graduate. No matter how interesting the material or how well it is taught, the fact that it is required is enough to make it hated by the student. The rationale of requirements is that teachers know better than students.[1] If there were no requirements, students would take only courses they enjoy and/or get good grades in, and the whole purpose of education (to learn to endure suffering) would be negated.

[1] Read aloud, this comes out "No better than students," which is what students think, when they are being generous.

Requisition. A written request, usually in triplicate, for essential supplies, such as a pencil, a piece of chalk, or the latest model computer. A requisition goes from one department to another until it finally reaches its destination, where it is lost (i.e., filed).

Resocialization. Learning a second culture, assuming one has been successful in initial socialization (learning one's own). Resocialization is also necessary for those who have been socialized to believe the policeman is the Bad Guy and the criminal is the Good Guy and must be shown movies (carefully chosen, else the original concepts will be reinforced) proving that it is the opposite. Resocialization is essential for students who are immigrants from, say, England, and refer to the hood of a car as a bonnet and a dessert as a trifle. Then there are those who grew up in a family stressing the importance of thrift who must be resocialized before they can fit into a society where there is no need to save, with Welfare ready to step in if the going gets hard.

Resource person. A person with special knowledge or experience who may be drawn upon (especially in art classes when they are out of paper) for information. Thus a local politician may be brought into a class in government or a convicted child molester into a class in sex education. Such persons may have a more first-hand and intimate knowledge of their profession than the teacher, who is inclined to be a generalist.[1]

Retirement. When a teacher at last has the time to do what he has always dreamed of doing but now is too

[1] Or, at Annapolis, an admiralist.

old to do it. At least he no longer has to take any guff from the principal (dean, head of the department), but gets to stay home and take it all day from his wife.[1]

Riot. Everyday disturbances, hardly noticed on some campuses, involving the use of tear gas and Mace by the police and bayonets by the National Guard. The students defend themselves as best they can with switchblades, Molotov cocktails, and crudely made time bombs, along with such diversionary tactics as setting fire to the Administration Building. Here is a nostalgic, simple-minded piece of verse, called "Born Too Soon," written by someone well over thirty and referred to these days as a "dinosaur":

[1] Fortunately, the children have grown up, so he doesn't have them to cope with. But he either worries about not hearing from them or owes them a letter.

When I was a student,
I was quiet.
I didn't protest,
I didn't riot.
I wasn't unwashed,
I wasn't obscene,
I made no demands
On prexy or dean.
I sat in no sit-in,
I heckled no speaker,
I broke not a window. . . .
Few students were meeker.
I'm forced to admit,
With some hesitation,
All I got out of school
Was an education.

The Situation Gets Out of Hand

Police Brutality

Attack of the Coeds

Tear Gas

The Arrest of the Martyr

Room mother. A spy for the PTA, disguised as a co-operative, compassionate mother. The room mother helps arrange Open House, Know-Your-Own-Teacher, and other parties so that members of the PTA can see with their own eyes what she has seen. "You wouldn't believe me, would you?" she asks triumphantly at the next PTA meeting. Among the things she had described to the horrified group: no paper towels in the washroom, galoshes not lined up, dust on the windowsill, and a suggestive bit of graffiti: "Tom loves Nancy." For her particularly outstanding work, she may be elected PTA president next year, or at least corresponding secretary.

Rorschach test. A test devised by the Swiss psychiatrist Hermann Rorschach, in which a person reveals his personality by looking at a series of ink blots and telling what each looks like to him. The same ink blot may look like a spider to one person, a shaggy dog to another, and to still another something that causes the person to blush deeply and refuse to say anything. The really abnormal person, full of frustrations and possibly psychotic, when asked what the ink blot resembles may blurt out something really wild, such as "An ink blot!" Such a person should be wrestled to the floor and pinioned by the school psychiatrist, if necessary with the help of the football coach. Then he should be put away somewhere.[1]

[1] You will remember what Lady Macbeth said: "Out, damned spot!" She was definitely crazy. How Professor Rorschach invented his test is not known, but he may have been brooding over an ink spot on his last clean shirt. And there he was, late for class already.

ROTC. Reserve Officers Training Corps (or, in some institutions, where the enrollment is dropping, Corpse). Called Rotsy by students. A program in Military Science, or the techniques of mass killing. It is a distinct improvement over individual killing, known as murder, which is not given academic credit. The ROTC is strenuously opposed by (1) persons opposed to war who think no one else is and (2) those who would prefer to have our military forces led by officers trained in the military academies and less inhibited by ethical concepts than officers with a liberal arts background. The student who signs up for ROTC is interested in having the salary and perquisites of an officer should he be impelled by patriotism to go forth and save his country. At some institutions credit is denied because Military Science is not as academic a subject as Rug Making or Advanced Badminton.[1]

Sabbatical. Just as the seventh day of the week is the Sabbath, or day of rest, the seventh year of teaching is a sabbatical, or year of rest. Anyone who is on a sabbatical is well advised to go abroad, where he can rest without being subjected to the envy of colleagues

[1] One college that has dropped credit for ROTC after violent demonstrations gives a course in Non-Violence.

not on a sabbatical. Resting in or near a library or museum is known as doing research.[1]

School bond. Indebtedness assumed, and indeed voted for, by taxpayers. Interest on school bonds is paid by taxpayers and their children and their children's children until the bonds reach maturity, which is later for bonds than for people. People who vote against school bonds usually own a great deal of property and have no children in school, in addition to which they are emotionally upset by reports that a teacher in the high school is a left-winger or anyhow sneezed during the Pledge of Allegiance. Such people are no doubt mindful of those wise words in the Bible (Ecclesiastes I, 18): "He that increaseth knowledge increaseth sorrow."

Seating chart. A plan showing where each student is seated in the classroom. Students are sometimes seated alphabetically, which means that a student named Charles Abbott will pay better attention, be called on more often, and therefore learn more than a student named Stanislaus Zlobotny.[2] But often students are seated so that they will not be close to friends with whom they will "socialize" or next to bright students from whom they will "crib." The teacher who works out such a seating chart is alert,

[1] Some think the sabbatical is connected with the seven-year itch, and a professor goes abroad so that his students will not see him scratching.

[2] The author will probably be sued by some genius named Stanislaus Zlobotny. Geniuses, however, have no business being in school. They don't need it, and they make it harder for the other students.

experienced, and mean. Being seated next to the prettiest girl in the class may make a boy's grades go down, but he is usually willing to pay the price.

Secondary school. The same as high school. The term secondary seems to have arisen from the fact that to many students and teachers at this level, school is a secondary consideration, having taken a back seat (see "Seating chart," above) to such things as sex (students) and money (teachers) or, with some, sex *and* money.

Self-image. How the student conceives of himself. He can make a beginning by looking into a mirror. Or he can try to overhear what other students are saying about him. This will give him something to compare with his own image, and there may be a few surprises. In what is called a "truth session," students sit around and say brutally frank things about one another. The advantage of the truth session, in developing one's self-image, is that it is not necessary to strain to overhear what is being said, and the student with poor hearing has an equal chance.

Semester. From the Latin *semestris*, half yearly, which in turn comes from *sex mensis*, which isn't what you are thinking. Originally it was a period of six months, but now it is one of the two periods of sixteen to eighteen weeks into which the academic year is divided, unless the institution is on the quarter system. The two semesters are fall and spring, and when a professor says he is "off" during the spring semester he doesn't mean that he is any different mentally during that period.[1] Anyhow, he is "on" again before he can find the time to write the first sentence of the book he was going to finish.

Seminar. From the Latin *semen, seminis,* seed, as is rarely mentioned. Presumably the professor plants seeds in the student's mind, though there is also cross-fertilization among the students. Some seeds fall on barren ground, or perhaps rocky craniums. In a seminar everyone is supposed to talk, though not all at once. Usually two or three students do most of the talking, hoping to get enough credit for "class participation" to make up for a skimpy term paper. Some professors lecture to a seminar just as they do to a large class, this being, as they say, the thing they do best.[2] The seminar may meet in the professor's home, and just as the intellectual level starts to rise a little, the professor's wife gets things back to normal by coming in with punch and cookies.

Sex education. Education in sex, usually by means of a course that explains the difference between boys and girls, and tells how babies are born. Unless the course is given at the pre-school level, students will already have learned it all from television, magazines, graffiti, and friends. However the course provides a review of basic principles for the instructor and is effective in arousing the indignation of parents who think sex should be taught in the home but never get around to it.

[1] A professor may even say, "I am off the whole year."
[2] I.e., the only thing they know how to do.

Sharing time. A time when students share things they have brought to school, such as a loaded revolver, a boa constrictor, or an appendix scar. The teacher asks searching questions, such as, "Where do you suppose that black widow spider could have gone?"

Show and tell. Much like "sharing time," except that the teacher is constantly on edge about what a student may show and what a student may tell about what he or she shows. It *does* give students a good chance to express themselves, and anyone who is skittish should stay out of teaching or teach at the college level, where this sort of thing, if it goes on at all, doesn't go on in the classroom. "Show and tell," by the way, should not be confused with "kiss and tell" or "American Tel and Tel."

Simulation. Also known as "role playing." The student learns by assuming a part, almost as if acting in a play. By pretending to be a Senator or Congressman, for instance, the student learns to be thoughtful about relatives, appointing them to easy jobs with high salaries. A student may even pretend to be a teacher. This is one of the most difficult roles, requiring the simulation of fatigue, frustration, and hopelessness. What the student learns from this is that there must be *some* better way of earning a living.

Slow learner. A term used by teachers when describing a failing student to parents. Euphemism for "stupid." Sometimes, however, a slow learner is simply a considerate child, reluctant to go faster than the teacher.[1]

Snap. An easy course. Subject to change, however. With a new instructor, half the class may fail. Students need to keep their information up to date.

Snap quiz. A quiz (see "Quiz," above) given in class without advance notice. Students consider this unfair, because it assumes that they have been doing the assignments regularly. Anyone knows[2] that extracurricular activities come first and make this impossible. The word "snap" in this usage probably derives from the snap of the teacher's fingers, or to something snapping in his brain.

[1] Genuinely slow learners are in a class by themselves. They also have their own teacher, someone who is being punished for cutting too many staff meetings.

[2] Anyone but a teacher, that is.

Socialized vocalization. Sounds made as a means of communication but not yet formed into actual words. Usually true of children at about five months of age, but seemingly true also of adolescents whose muttering can be understood only by other adolescents. Folk-rock singers, popular with students, specialize in nonverbal communication which, to adults, is anti-social as well as un-American.

Society-centered school. A school where the curriculum is more concerned with the needs of society than with the needs of the individual student. In a finishing school, where the tuition is high, the curriculum is centered on high society. The purpose of education in a society-centered school is to make the student a cog in the machine or, if possible, a Big Wheel. The emphasis is on the need for people to live together harmoniously, no matter how many to a room.

Socio-economic approach. Studies approached with one eye to the social and one eye to economics. This approach has produced more wall-eyed students than is desirable.[1]

Speed reading. A method of teaching a slow reader to read *War and Peace* or *Paradise Lost* in a matter of minutes. He takes longer to fill out the order card for a book than to read it, and uses a wheelbarrow to carry enough books from the library to last until the next day. If a speed reader cannot remember what

[1] The ideal teacher using the socio-economic approach is a sociologist who is married to an economist. They may sleep in separate bedrooms, but their conversation is stimulating and they have a fusion of interests.

he has read, he can (and will) tell you his precise reading rate in words per minute, at which you are supposed to exclaim, "Amazing!" or "Incredible!" There is no evidence that Aristotle, Confucius, Einstein, and Rockefeller were speed readers.[1]

Sprachgefühl. A German word meaning feeling for language. A student who has *Sprachgefühl* gets good grades in foreign language courses without half trying and is envied and resented by the other students. "I just don't have *Sprachgefühl*," says a student who is flunking Elementary German, and the way he mispronounces the word makes the professor wince. The professor has *Sprachgefühl* for German, having been born in Munich, but very little for English.

Stacks. An area in the library where books are not stacked on top of one another, as you might think, but are lined up on shelves as elsewhere. Open stacks are stacks that anyone, even students, may enter. In some schools, stacks are closed because the librarian cannot double as a chaperone.[2]

Staff meeting. A meeting of the principal, teachers, and others to consider school problems. Its equivalent at the college or university level is a faculty meeting, which also takes longer than it should. Such meetings if regularly scheduled may have no business whatever to dispose of, in which case they last still longer.

[1] Of course Rockefeller had to be a speed *counter* to keep up with his money.

[2] A well-stacked library is not to be confused with a well-stacked librarian.

Stencil. Everyone knows what this is, so why define it? As Ogden Nash might have written:

> In schools a stencil
> Is indispencil.

Stockroom. Also called a storeroom. A room used for storing educational and janitorial supplies that either does not contain what is urgently needed or is locked. In wealthy suburban schools there may be so much audiovisual equipment that the stockroom is a separate building, a warehouse. Teachers drawing out equipment show their driver's license and their credit cards, fill out a requisition in triplicate, and take a lie detector test after an injection of truth serum. Meanwhile the principal is watching by closed-circuit television, partly to see that everything is in order and partly to run a screen test before casting the faculty play.

Strike. What teachers and other faithful public servants never do.[1]

Structured. Planned, organized, or giving the appearance thereof. A curriculum is said to be structured if there is a meaningful progression, going methodically from A to Z or, more likely, from A to B. There are also structured tests, structured inventories, structured interviews, and, with reference to buildings, structured structures. "Unstructured" is often used as a synonym, in educational circles, for "utter shambles."

Student union. (1) A building for student activities,

[1] This definition was taken from a book published in 1913.

such as eating. (2) An organization of students, usually having some such laudable aim as taking over the functions of the faculty, administration, and trustees.

Study hall. A room used by students for napping, writing notes to each other, making humorous sketches of the teacher in charge, and otherwise preparing for the next class.

Subliminal instruction. Classes held in the basement.

Substitute teacher. A teacher who temporarily replaces a teacher who is absent. The substitute teacher, being unfamiliar with the lesson material and merely trying to pass the time, is popular with students, who hate to have the regular teacher return. A teacher who misses classes two days spends at least a week getting the class back on the track. The substitute teacher, who is paid by the day, is always hoping for a good flu epidemic. But sometimes the substitute teacher catches the bug, and that leaves it to the substitute substitute teacher, or sub sub.[1]

Summer vacation. The most important fringe benefit of teaching. For three blissful months, every day is like Saturday or Sunday. Some teachers spoil their vacation by taking summer school work and spoil the vacations of others by telling them how much more they will earn because of these additional credits. Teachers who don't take summer school work get a certain satisfaction out of sending flowers, along

[1] "We'll have to scrape up *somebody*," the principal says. Scraping up a teacher is no fun, and the teacher who has been scraped up usually looks it.

about the next February, to a teacher who took summer school work and is now suffering a physical and mental breakdown.

Superintendent. A person with dictatorial power over principals and teachers (taking the "super" literally), who reveals such traits as humility and obsequiousness only when appearing before the School Board. If the superintendent possesses a rugged physique, with hairy forearms and a bull neck, this may be because of his years working on a road gang and then as a football coach before assuming the superintendency.[1]

[1] A little over half of the word "superintendency," we should point out, is "tendency." "Tendency to what?" you may ask. That depends largely on the superintendent.

Supervisory classroom visit. The principal, vice-principal, or someone else with the authority to recommend promotion or pay increases drops into a class unexpectedly and asks, when he can be heard over the din, "How are things going?" If, just as he enters the room, he is hit in the face by a flying eraser, (1) he doesn't need to ask, (2) it serves him right, (3) it indicates he has lost rapport.[1] (Check one.)

Survey course. A course that covers everything and uncovers or discovers very little. An example is Western Civilization, referred to by students as Western Civ or, considering the way it runs through them, Western Sieve. There is also English Survey, a course that begins with the *Beowulf* and comes up to the Present, the period since 1914 being covered in the final lecture. The idea behind the survey course is that it is better to know something about everything important than everything about something unimportant, the latter being left to the doctoral dissertation.

Suspension. The state of being suspended, or hung. Unlike the bad man in a Western or a side of beef, a student who is suspended is not actually hung, or hanged, though there are members of the faculty and administration who wish this were the case. The student is merely asked (told) to withdraw temporarily, and the chances are, alas, that he will be back. Suspension instead of expulsion is the penalty applied by those in authority who have some courage but not enough.[2]

[1] When he got up that morning, he asked his wife distractedly, "Now what *did* I do with my rapport?"

[2] An even more cautious penalty is suspended suspension.

Teacher of the year. A person chosen as the outstanding teacher of a school, city, state, or even the nation. Choice of the Teacher of the Year is an excellent way to make some teacher feel appreciated and to make thousands of others jealous. Balloting for Teacher of

the Year has been found riddled with irregularities and fraud, comparable to the average election in Southeast Asia. But after all, the prize is so great that the end may justify the meanness.

Teachers' club. If a teacher has one, he had better seek legal advice before using it on a student.

Teachers' institute. A conference of teachers to discuss educational problems. Attendance is usually quite good, especially if required. Most teachers consider attending an institute preferable to teaching. You can sleep through somebody else's lecture but not your own.

Teaching assistant. Also known as a T.A. The lowest-ranking member of the faculty of a college or university. Such a person is limited to assisting in introductory courses forming the foundation for all subsequent courses in the field, with influence only upon establishing basic attitudes and habits of research. Not being eligible for a sabbatical, and not being able to afford a car, the teaching assistant is always available to students. If he is not in his office,[1] he may be found in the library working on his dissertation, which is going slowly because of his teaching and his moonlighting as an attendant in a service station.

Team teaching. Teaching by a group of teachers who by pooling their knowledge know enough to teach a course, if it is not too advanced. Teachers who are members of such a unit develop team spirit and cheer each other through such difficult times as the opening of the school year, the middle of the school year, and the end of the school year. One thing about team teaching: if the course goes badly, the blame can be shared. Each teacher blames the others. Recently offensive and defensive teams have been introduced, depending on who has (or is on) the ball.

[1] Which does double duty as a telephone booth.

122

Tenure. What a teacher has that enables him to keep his job no matter how miserably he teaches.[1] Once a teacher gains tenure he can breathe easily. In fact all he needs to do is to keep breathing until he reaches the age of retirement. Very few are aware that "tenure" comes from the French *tenir*, to hold, and is akin to "tenor," a person who holds a note for a long time and up high. Historically, tenure goes back to the Middle Ages and refers to the holding of property, which was something a serf couldn't do. When a teacher with tenure begins to feel like a serf, especially around parents, he should keep this in mind.

Test. An examination, somewhat longer and harder than a quiz. For name-droppers, tests include the Meier-Seashore test of art judgment, the Kwalwasser-Dykema music test, the Holmgren wool test for color blindness, the von Pirquet tuberculin test, the Rosenzweig picture-frustration test, and the Purdue pegboard test for finger dexterity.[2] The Rosenzweig pic-

[1] With a woman teacher it may be sex appeal.

[2] Nor should we forget the Wassermann test. Students and teachers who get a clean bill of health on this one have a right to be relieved, swearing to be more careful in the future.

123

ture-frustration test is not, as one might suppose, a test of the frustration suffered by a student trying to figure out the meaning of an abstract painting. It is, rather, a series of drawings of people being frustrated by something or other involving their ego or super-ego, and the student is supposed to figure out what it is. Efforts to determine what is to be gained by this test have been unavailing, and this leads to the kind of frustration Rosenzweig may have had in mind. On the subject of tests, we should not overlook the Spear-man-Brown prophecy formula, a formula for esti-mating the reliability of a test. This formula can, if you insist upon it, be written:

$$r_n = \frac{nr12}{1 + (n-1)r12},$$

where r_n represents the reliability coefficient of a test n times as long as it should be. According to the Spearman-Brown prophecy (both men looked into the same crystal ball), the test will be reasonably reliable, no matter what its length, if the same test is given year after year and students can buy a mimeographed copy of the answers at a reasonable price.

Textbook. A book that is required in a course, often by the professor who wrote it. If possible, a student buys a secondhand copy, not only because it is cheaper but because the important words and sen-tences are already underlined and there may even be some interesting comments and drawings in the mar-gins. Below the college level, adoption of a textbook is somewhat more difficult than adoption of a child, involving authorization by the School Board and perhaps by the State Department of Education. Even then, parents complain that the textbook is biased, i.e., has a bias different from their own. When parents say a textbook is inspired, they mean Communist-inspired. Changing from one textbook to another is especially hard on teachers, who are forced to read another book.

Thesis. A piece of written work longer than a term paper but shorter than a dissertation. Technically, a thesis has a thesis; that is, it attempts to prove something or it takes a position, such as standing, sitting, kneeling, or, most often, prone or supine. Sometimes the student is asked to defend his thesis, armed only with a ballpoint pen. Few students will go so far as Martin Luther, who nailed ninety-five theses on the door of All Saints' Church in Wittenberg instead of submitting them in the regular way, in spring binders.[1] A thesis is usually due on or before a certain day, which to a student is always several weeks too soon.

Three r's. Reading, riting, and rithmetic. See the expression, "He doesn't know his r's from a hole in the ground."

Training. A low form of education in which students actually learn how to do something.

Transfer student. A college student who has transferred from another institution for reasons never fully dis-

[1] It is no wonder that Luther (who also burned the Pope's bull in the public square) was imprisoned and forced to live on a diet of worms.

closed. The transfer student usually has a certain number of credits which are not, as he is, transferable, and he is therefore forced to remain an extra year before graduating or (a fate worse than death) to take work in summer school. He is bitter about this, blaming the previous institution for permitting him to take the courses he insisted on taking and the institution to which he has transferred for not accepting such courses for credit. However he soon becomes more loyal to the new institution than those who have been there from the start and have grown tired of it. After graduation, the transfer student is a soft touch for fund raisers, who have only to hum the "Alma Mater" in his presence to reduce him to tears and check writing.

Trichopathophobia. Undue concern about hair. This unfortunate condition is widespread among adolescents in junior high school and high school. It takes the form, in boys, of carefully counting and noting

the growth of hairs on the chest. With girls it involves the plucking and shaping, replucking and reshaping, of the eyebrows. With the advent of wigs and false eyelashes, girls have a vastly wider range of hair anxieties. Meanwhile boys, growing their hair longer, must decide whether to tuck it under their collar, in what shape to trim their sideburns, and what style of moustache and/or beard to cultivate.

Teachers, principals, and parents must decide at what point this thing (hair) has gone too far, and whether they are willing to do battle with the American Civil Liberties Union. Salk vaccine has virtually done away with poliomyelitis, and a cure for cancer is on its way, but trichopathophobia has reached epidemic proportions. Some analysts of the educational scene consider this the Age of the Follicle.

Trivium. In the Middle Ages the trivium consisted of the three basic studies: grammar, rhetoric, and dialectic. Now the curriculum has been extended to include the trivia: basket weaving, cake decorating, and square dancing.[1]

Truant officer. The word "truant" can be traced back to the Gaelic *truaghan*, a poor, distressed, or wretched creature. A truant officer is the educational equivalent of a dog catcher.[2]

Trustee. A member of the Board of Trustees of a school or college, entrusted with overall policies. Actually trustees are concerned with more than overalls or even mini-skirts. For years they seemed primarily concerned with leftist tendencies. Lately riots have attracted their attention. Trustees are men of trust, often heads of trust companies. They are wealthy, tend to be men of affairs,[3] sit on lots of boards, and are much too busy to look into inconsequential mat-

[1] One rule about the trivia: the lower the academic value, the easier to get a high grade.

[2] The truant officer we are talking about is an officer who catches truants, and not an officer who has run away from the force.

[3] This does not mean that *all* of them have affairs.

ters such as the competence of teaching and the relevance[1] of the curriculum. A trustee's viewpoint is usually as different from a student's as possible, which some educators think makes for balance and others for trouble.

Tuition. From the Latin *tueri, tuitus, tutus,* to watch, guard, protect. Some etymologists find it akin to the Gothic *thiuth,* that which is good, though the Goth who coined it may merely have had a lithp. In its current meaning, "tuition" refers to that which is good and expensive.

Unassigned period. (1) A period that has not yet been assigned to a sentence it hopes some day to end. (2) A time when the student is free to pursue work of his own choosing. A survey of 100 junior-high-school students during an unassigned period revealed the following use being made of the time:

[1] The all-purpose word of the post-McLuhan period.

Reading unassigned works (after all, this is an unassigned period), such as *Playboy*, *Secret True Confessions*, and *Mad*   12

Filing nails   3

Examining teeth in a mirror   1

Squeezing a pimple   1

Eating a candy bar   5

Drinking Coke (while eating candy bar)   5

Sleeping (with eyes closed)   7

Sleeping (with eyes open)   66

Underclassman. A member of the freshman or sophomore class. One who looks up to an upperclassman. (See "Upperclassman.")

Unexcused absence. Absence without an excuse, showing lack of resourcefulness on the part of the student. When Thomas Haynes Bayly (1797–1839) wrote in *Isle of Beauty* that "Absence makes the heart grow fonder," he could hardly have been thinking of an unexcused absence.[1]

Unit. A basic measure of academic credit. A three-unit course takes three times as much of a student's time as a one-unit course, and the student should therefore learn exactly three times as much. Education is measured in units, just as liquids are measured in pints, quarts, and gallons (also fifths). If a student is one unit short of the requirement for graduation, he does not graduate, because he is just that much short of being educated. By means of the unit system educators measure the unmeasurable.[2]

University. From the Latin *universitas*, all together, the whole, the universe. A university, therefore, is where you are likely to find almost anything. Unlike a college, a university is empowered to confer advanced degrees in such fields as animal husbandry and midwifery. There are state universities and private universities. Both have their worries: the state university has its narrow-minded legislators and the private university has its tightwad alumni. In the private university the president sometimes has to play politics. In the state university he doesn't play—it's the real thing.

[1] By the way, the next line of Bayly's poem, not so widely quoted, is "Isle of Beauty, fare thee well!"

[2] An embarrassing mistake is sometimes made in conversation, as when the Sultan said, "I need three extra eunuchs," and everyone thought he planned to go back to school.

Unstructured. Education that is without plan, permitting everyone freedom of choice. *Syn.* "chaotic." The teacher or administrator who wishes to avoid criticism for failing to organize, prepare, or foresee should keep this word in mind. If he can look at overturned desks and broken windows and say coolly and confidently, "Unstructured, you know," he is destined for bigger things in the field of education.

Upperclassman. A member of the junior or senior class. One who looks down on an underclassman. (See "Underclassman.")

Variable. Something that varies, is inconstant, such as a teacher's disposition and his attitude toward remaining in the teaching profession. Among the variables which will not be explained here[1] are the concomitant variable, the predictive variable, the discontinuous variable, and the suppressor variable, which is not as bad as it sounds. There is also the game, Animal, Variable, and Mineral.

[1] Shrewd authors save things for their next book, thus keeping their publishers and their readers in suspense.

Venereal disease. The high point of any course in sex education.

Veritas. A word used in mottoes and inscriptions in order to keep Latin in the curriculum.

Vice-president. A person who is only a heartbeat from the presidency of a college or university, and that bulge in his pocket is a stethoscope. The vice-president for academic affairs is in charge of faculty affairs, the ones involving vice. This kind of work keeps him on his toes.[1]

Visual aids. Motion pictures, slides, overhead projectors, and other devices to help the teacher when words fail. Problems frequently encountered with visual aids are that they are (1) being used by someone else, (2) misplaced, or (3) broken.

Vita. A brief autobiography, including, for lack of space, only what is favorable and calculated to impress. Used with equal effectiveness in either an application or an obituary.

Vocational education. Education for a vocation, the word "vocation" deriving from the Latin *vocare*, to call, hence a calling. Two kinds of students find the call hard to hear: the deaf and the lazy. Vocational education is looked down upon by intellectuals who, without the aid of those vocationally trained, would have to sit around helplessly with their finger in a broken water pipe and the TV set not working.[2]

[1] Peeking through transoms.
[2] A nice expression, accidentally coined through a typographical error, is "vacational education," gained by reading travel circulars.

Weight. A factor used in calculating the teaching load, involving such considerations as time needed to prepare for a single period of instruction, difficulty of the subject, and resistance on the part of students. When you hear a teacher say, "I'm putting on weight," it probably has nothing to do with the teaching load.

Well adjusted. A student or teacher who is able to get along well with society and with himself. *Rare.*

Wherry-Doolittle multiple correlation test selection method. A method invented by Wherry and Doolittle for multiple correlation test selection.[1]

Whole-part-whole method. Analytic-synthetic method of teaching reading, to be distinguished from the whole method and the part method. One who understands the whole-part-whole method is so far advanced that further study, or even reading, is unnecessary.

Withdrawal. (1) Dropping out of a course before a specified date, thus avoiding failure. Also known as "copping out," a mixture of cowardice and caution. (2) Retreating into oneself, becoming antisocial. In the case of a girl student, this type of withdrawal is often caused by discovery that a handsome bachelor teacher is getting married during spring vacation.

[1] Any questions? Write Wherry or Doolittle.

Word association. Spontaneous, unthinking response to a word. A student may, for example, be given the word "teacher," and the immediate, unthinking response may be "mean" or "fat." If the student has been frequently subjected to testing, and the teacher who comes to mind is rather shapeless, the response may be "Rorschach."[1]

Xerox. A process for duplicating that is a very good thing, especially for stockholders in the Xerox Corporation. "Run off a few copies," the superintendent tells his secretary without saying how many. If it looks like something important, say the superintendent's talk to the Rotary Club, "You and Your School System," she runs off two hundred copies. After trying his best, the superintendent manages to get thirty-seven people to carry off copies.[2] That leaves one hundred and sixty-three copies to store somewhere and is a modest beginning toward making a case for a larger office and a second filing clerk.

[1] The unthinking response to questions is not, unfortunately, limited to word association.

[2] As far as their wastebasket.

XYZ grouping. Also known as tripartite grouping. Pupils are divided into three graded sections according to their ability. X is fast, Y is average, and Z is slow. When children come home and excitedly tell their parents, "I got put into X," parents may be excused for not at first sharing their enthusiasm, thinking the reference is to solitary confinement, dunce's corner, or something else the child is reluctant to name. One thing about the Z group: at least you cannot go any lower.

Yale frustration-aggression hypothesis. Not limited to Yale, and not an hypothesis but a fact. To wit: If anyone is repeatedly kept from doing what he wants to do, he becomes aggressive. Thus a teacher who tries to explain something in class but is continually interrupted by a student who has discovered his desk top squeaks and delightedly squeaks it despite repeated warnings, may march down the aisle, yank the student to his feet, and haul him off to the principal's office. "Either you give this kid a thrashing or I resign," the teacher says, up to the neck in frustration-aggressiveness. The odd thing is that students, even if they have not heard of the Yale hypothesis, know the consequences of interrupting the teacher, and yet keep right on doing it. This is called masochism.[1]

Yearbook. Also known as an "annual," inasmuch as it comes out every year. That is, unless funds are insufficient, the editor resigns late in the spring, or the book is confiscated by the administration because of pornographic writing and suggestive photos. When they receive their yearbooks, students take them around to have their friends write in the margins such witty or sentimental remarks as "Good to have known you," "Be seeing you," and "Hi!" It is in the yearbook that the Student Most Likely to Succeed is announced. If he succeeds, he forgets about this prediction and loses his yearbook. If, through some unhappy misadventure, he ends up in State Prison, his yearbook is always on the shelf above his bed. It gives him solace and something to do, thumbing through those yellowed pages while he awaits eligibility for parole and the chance to attend a class reunion.

Yo-he-ho theory. The theory that language originated with the spontaneous vocalizations of primitive man while engaged in cooperative projects such as lifting a large stone or turning over a dead mammoth. Of course, Yo, He, and Ho may have been the names of three Stone Age men whom a fourth man, perhaps named Hum, exploited. "Yo, He, Ho, lend me hand," he would say, and then stand to one side, encouraging them, as they tugged, strained, and brought on hernias.[2]

[1] What it sometimes leads to is called murder.
[2] Does Hum remind you of anyone? Some school administrator, perhaps, getting three insecure teachers to move the piano in the recreation room?

Youth problem. A problem caused by school-age young people. The problem would not exist if people could go directly from infancy to adulthood or, even better, be born old. Another solution would be if everyone could be young, since the youth problem is a problem only for old people (i.e., over thirty). The chief purpose of our school system is not to educate but to keep young people away from old people, except teachers,[1] as much as possible. As young people say, when they are among themselves, "What's the problem?"

Zaner-Bloser handwriting system. A system of writing very large until third grade and then starting to write smaller. Fortunately, the writing doesn't get smaller and smaller from then on, or teachers would have to read the papers of high-school seniors through a jeweler's glass. If older teachers think the handwriting of their students is getting smaller and smaller, they shouldn't blame Zaner and Bloser. They should get some new glasses.

[1] Or keepers.

Zero transfer. Transfer of absolutely none of the information and skills learned in one discipline to another. Proving a zero transfer, according to educational psychologists, involves proving a null hypothesis, and proving a null hypothesis is said to be impossible. It is safer, therefore, to refer to "almost zero transfer." "Almost," in this instance, is a weasel word, picked up while listening to a conversation between two weasels.[1]

Zoanthropy. The delusion of having been changed into an animal. This is usually temporary, as when a first-grader says, with appropriate gestures and grimaces, "Look, I'm a bear" and the next minute shouts, "Look, I'm an elephant!" It is more lasting and disturbing when a teacher has a recurrent nightmare that she is a frightened little rabbit being chased by a ravenous old wolf that bears a curious resemblance to the school principal. As the teacher (rabbit) tries to get away, she finds her escape blocked by a pack of evil little foxes, their fangs bared, that look for all the world like her students. She wakes up screaming. After enough nights of such zoanthropy, the teacher asks for transfer to another school or gives up teaching for a less nightmarish profession, perhaps becoming a cashier at a movie theater[2] or a carhop at a drive-in[3]

[1] If you are an educational psychologist, it helps to have things like "zero transfer" and "null hypothesis" to mutter when you want to be overheard muttering professionally.

[2] With higher financial responsibilities than collecting milk money.

[3] After all, did anybody ever tip a teacher?

Abbreviations

Most of these abbreviations have not been used, but a dictionary would seem incomplete without such a list.

abbr., abbreviation for "abbreviation."

awf., awful, something the reader may wish to write in the margin.

B.A., Bachelor of Agriculture or bloody awful, especially in British usage.

ba, bachelor, sometimes spelled bah.

b.f., bold face, referring either to a type or to a type of person found in educational circles.

cat., catalogue, or the word "cat" at the end of a sentence.

chmn., chairman, sometimes written ch---man, since it is a dirty word.

D.D.D., *dono dedit, dedicavit* (Latin for he gave and consecrated as a gift), or Doctor, Doctor, Doctor, a doctor's degree given to a donor.

dpt., department, with all of the vowels removed, there having been an order to cut down.

d.w., dead weight, used with reference to certain school administrators.

ff., not the grade but the Latin *fecerunt*, they did it, or a runt did it, used when a teacher doesn't wish to name names.

gr., grammar, also the sound made by an English teacher upon encountering a grammatical error.

MGM, not Metro-Goldwyn-Mayer but Mentally Gifted Minors, referring to students with an IQ of 130 or better. EMR are the Educable Mentally Retarded (IQ of below 79) and TMR are the Trainable Mentally Retarded (IQ of below 60). Lower than that, words and abbreviations fail.

syn., synonym. There is also original syn, as is pointed out in courses in Religion.

typ., typist. Also, and as often, typographical error.

wk., week, spelled weak when referring to a teacher after five days of it.

About the Author

Though he is best known for his writing of humor and satire, Richard Armour began his career as a serious scholar. A graduate of Pomona College and a Ph.D. from Harvard, he has taught for nearly forty years in many colleges and universities (moving voluntarily, especially after he gained tenure), has held research fellowships in France and England, and has lectured or been guest-in-residence on more than 200 campuses. He has also lectured as an American Specialist for the State Department in both Europe and Asia. After producing enough scholarly books of biography and literary criticism to become a full professor, he turned to the writing of such books as *It All Started with Columbus, Twisted Tales from Shakespeare*, and *The Classics Reclassified*, which have sold over a million copies and have been hailed as "Some of the sprightliest satire in many a moon" (*The New York Times*), "Wicked and witty, funny as the devil" (*Chicago Tribune*), and "Uninhibited, unlicensed, and unexcelled" (*St. Louis Post-Dispatch*). This is his fortieth book. Dr. Armour is thoroughly at home with education and educators. Some of his best friends are (or were) teachers, and students have long been the most enthusiastic readers of his irreverent spoofs of history and literature. He is married, has a son and daughter who provided him with the material for his *Through Darkest Adolescence*, and lives in Claremont, California.